Constance Hall lives "down south" in W her new husband Denim, four children, two stepchildren and a menagerie of animals.

She went viral with a blog post about "parent sex" a little over two years ago, and within a few days jumped from 2000 followers to over 200,000. She now has over 1.2 million followers on Facebook and over 280,000 on Instagram. Both these numbers grow month on month.

It's been an amazing success story with no signs of slowing down. Constance still gets loads of press – print, radio and TV interviews – and is seen as a sometimes controversial, but always bluntly honest, blogger. Although Constance is referred to as a "mummy blogger", a proportion of her followers (her "Queens") do not have children. She is currently the co-host on the national radio show *The Queen Sesh with Constance Hall and Annaliese* and has her own "all sizes" clothing label, *Queen the Label*.

Still a Queen is her follow-up memoir to the bestselling *Like a Queen*.

Also by Constance Hall

Like a Queen

More by Constance Hall

Facebook: /mrsconstancehall
Instagram: @mrsconstancehall

CONSTANCE HALL

STILL A QUEEN

HOUSE OF QUEENS PUBLISHING

First published in 2018

Copyright © Constance Hall, 2018

Published by House of Queens Publishing
Email: publishing@houseofqueens.com.au
www.houseofqueens.com.au

Cover Photographs by Frances Andrjich Photography.
Second Camera: Clair Negri
Cover Design by: Christabella Designs
Printed by CanPrint Communications
Still a Queen
Hall, Constance

ISBN 9780648244707

This book is dedicated to you, the Queens, who have supported me, allowing me to do this on my own, to write for a living and support my family.

You are the ones responsible for the change in this world. Just by reading this self-published book, whether borrowed or bought, it found you because you are a Queen. Collectively we have become one giant middle finger extended to the system, a "fuck you" to the world that said we cannot.

Because we can.

CONTENTS

A NOTE TO MY READERS

In order to maintain the anonymity of people mentioned in *Still a Queen*, I have changed the names of some individuals and places.

Please be aware there is profanity, mention of drug use, suicide, mental health issues, miscarriage, abortion, eating disorders and bullying. Some of these topics may be upsetting. I don't profess to be an expert with any advice I've given and if you have any serious issues or concerns please contact a professional, or at least talk to a friend.

I know some of you will want to read about the reasons why my marriage fell apart, but out of respect for my ex-husband and concern for our children, I have chosen not to discuss this in *Still a Queen*. It is between their father and I. There are always two sides in a breakdown of a relationship and my children don't ever need to read either point of view.

STILL A QUEEN

A lot of things have happened; to me, to you, to everyone. Beautiful things, terrible things, and shameful things.

I sat in a bar in London, waiting to meet a friend. My computer and mind were consumed with a novel I was writing for young adults. Fiction was my escape, since I had recently become Australia's most hated woman. My rise and fall had been very quick. I had enjoyed a short time of carefree success before I had become too big for some, and was sliced down and witch-hunted. Then the unspeakable happened – I dared to get a new boyfriend.

The bar was a hipster spot, and while attractive people in weird, uncomfortable-looking clothes swanned in and out, I sat almost hidden in the corner.

A bubbly woman asked me for a photograph and told me she loved me. I faked a smile and told her I loved her too. She kissed me on the cheek and left. I couldn't even hide in London.

I continued to think about my novel. My main character wasn't fat or thin, was extroverted and vulnerable, had a vulgar sense of humour and loved dick jokes... yep, she was a young me, and she took me to a place that didn't exist, where Constance Hall didn't exist. Or maybe just a place where Constance Hall wasn't scrutinised, called a slut, called a pig, asked to kill herself, ganged up on, embarrassed, and constantly told that she isn't a Queen.

A place where Constance Hall wasn't googling symptoms and convinced she was having a nervous breakdown.

My friend walked in: dark red lipstick, black jumpsuit, and blonde hair tied back; she looked like an approachable Charlize Theron and glowed with magical authenticity when she opened her mouth.

Taryn works in PR. She's a women's advocate, a married lesbian mother who works with some of the world's biggest names, and started a company called the Women's Collective to inspire and support women all over the world. Taryn not only has time for everyone, she studies them. In the space of one conversation, she makes you feel so well understood you could take on the world.

"What are you doing, woman? Tell me everything. I want to know it all. Tell me about your next book."

I proceeded to tell her about my new young adult novel. I was twenty thousand words in and quite proud of it so far.

We laughed, showed each other photos, talked fannies and relationships, professed how much we missed each other, and of course I explained in grave detail how it now feels to be a chubby, bogan D-grade celebrity with bad hair who everyone wants to see burned at the stake. She looked at me and said, "It's not the right time."

"For what?"

"For a novel. I'm sorry, I know you're into it but it's not right. It feels dishonest, it feels like you're hiding. It feels like you've been told to get back in your box and you've agreed. You, Con, need to *reclaim your right to be you*. Because everything that you have been through is human. We love you because you're human and we want to know what happened, we want you to give us the details about your life that you used to give us so candidly. You

4

don't write to the people who hate you, you write to the people who love you, people like me."

And then and there, surrounded by hipsters, I had a moment of clarity. She was right. Writing about my life *is* my right. Fiction is beautiful, and one day I'll return to that book. But right now, I'm here and I have so much more to say.

When I needed courage while writing this book, it was Taryn's face I visualised, because I'm writing to people who love me. People like her, and people like you.

And guess what?

Constance Hall has been a slut, very often looks feral, and is more often than not a massive pig. And she actually has considered killing herself over the bullying and trolling she has been subjected to, only to pull herself back from the edge.

I have never pretended to be anything other than a royal fuck-up.

But one thing they got wrong. She sure as shit is still a fucking Queen.

*

What do you think makes it so hard for women to succeed in this world? What makes the boys' club so strong? What keeps holding us back? What is keeping us at the fucking sink, while our male equivalents are sipping cognac on Chesterfields? It's our lack of sisterhood. We are holding each other back.

We must accept our power. This movement is already happening; the power of the woman is in full swing. I see it happening all the time. My readers are only here because they want to support each other and they want to support me. Perfect strangers choose to message each other support; they send each other gifts. As a reader you are here because *you* are part of this movement, *you* are the change.

We have learnt to shut the fuck up when that little voice that's embedded into our psyche says something bitchy or jealous. That voice is the patriarchy dividing us, and the more we ignore it, the more it disappears. There is room for us all and we will only get there together.

Terrible things happen to us. We do fucked-up things, we are bitches and people we have trusted turn out to be cunts. Women message me constantly, telling me that their crowns have slipped, that they are no longer Queens. But that is just not true. You are glorious, magnificent, strong and powerful. It's time we all reclaimed each other, and ourselves.

I am a canceller. I cancel coffees and drinks and phone chats all the time but it's time to stop. It's time to connect, to show the world how beautiful and unapologetic and connected with other women we are. I can't imagine where I'd be if I had cancelled and not connected with Taryn that day in London. Well, I'd probably be rocking in my wardrobe not taking calls, penning my fictional novel.

I receive thousands of messages a week from Queens who don't feel adequate.

I don't give a fuck who you are or what you've done. I want you to know that you are, and I am, STILL A QUEEN.

DUMB BITCH CAN'T SPELL

IT'S THEY'RE, NOT THEIR!

A lot of people are amazed that I don't have my blogs edited, and my mixed grammar, spelling and typos are still constantly pointed out, even after all this time. The thing is, if you point out someone's grammar or spelling mistakes publicly, you will probably sound like an arse.

> It's "women"... not "woman"... am I missing something? It's not rocket science.

Even the kinder ones:

> I'm not trying to be a bitch, but it really irks me to see these spelling mistakes.

Direct messages always sound a lot kinder – chicks write to me because they have identified a typo or spelling fuck-up and want to help me, not to be the hero or to publicly embarrass me:

> Babe, you wrote dick instead of click. Go, go, go and fix, girlfriend!!!

The funny thing? While all these people are completely freaking out for me, cringing gratefully that it isn't them fucking up in front of millions of people, I couldn't give two fucks. Seriously, I don't care. It is literally impossible to embarrass me over the notion that I am "dumb".

Do you know why? It's been there my whole life.

I have never been able to concentrate. Even writing this sentence I have literally looked at my phone, the time, the weather, my inbox, and stared out the window. I have even offered Denim a headjob to get out of finishing whatever it is I'm supposed to be concentrating on, and we all know how much pregnant chicks like penises down their throats.

I just can't focus or retain information. It's not the way my brain is wired.

When I was in Year 1, I was able to fly under the radar. Nobody expects much of a five-year-old so I stuck to myself. I wrote a poorly spelt "fuk scool" on my arm in permanent marker and had to sit in the corner for an entire day with my back to the class, "because nobody wants to see your face!" But that really had more to do with early signs of me being anti-establishment than being "dumb".

In Year 2, however, we were expected to read the kinds of books that my son is expected to read in pre-primary now. What a scary thought. I hope in thirty years we won't be expecting two-year-olds to speak four languages.

I just couldn't do it. It was the beginning of the feeling I have always had since, that I had missed something, like the day where everyone learnt to read. Or like now when I go to Facebook in summer and everyone's on a boat, and I'm like, "Fuck, was I out of town the day they handed out boats?"

My primary school was filled with pretty privileged kids; kids from straight backgrounds, kids whose parents were not only still together, but were professionals. This wasn't the norm for a kid who was wearing a second-hand school jumper, who was staying at her uncle's house with her very young mum and catching two buses and a train to school while her mum looked for another rental and job; whose parents were ex-drug addicts and had separated early.

I stood out like a sore thumb, partly because most of the dads and teachers wanted a crack at my mum, and partly because we just didn't "fit in". I never knew why none of the parents were friends with my mum. Now that I know a lot more about the class system of these areas and those times, I'm glad my mum always protected me from it.

My mum always made sure I looked neat, which I'm grateful for. In all the pictures, my hair is braided and my clothes are clean, and I have memories of my mum fixing my bed every night, getting every grain of sand off it before I jumped in. While people speculate on what it might be like to be raised by a young, single, spunky woman who had a taste for bad boys in rock bands, they would be wrong. What she lacked in funds, she made up for in a high standard of care for her children.

But that didn't stop the parent helpers and teachers from not being particularly surprised that I couldn't read.

We had a notebook with lines that was designed to keep track of the books we had to read, one per night. We had to write in the title of the book and have it signed. Everyone was getting second and third pages stapled into their books while I was still on my first page, and it did not have a single book title in it. I would line up in the mornings to show my teacher, and every single morning I would make an excuse: I needed to go to the toilet or get a drink, and I'd run off to hide my book under the pigeonholes, dreading the day it would be found and everyone would laugh their heads off at the fact that I couldn't read.

Looking back, of course they knew; they just didn't care. I wasn't the student to care about. I wasn't the one with anything to lose, so they let me get away with my lie.

My best friend, Annaliese, was the only person I told. She used to try and teach me. In Year 3, I would stay at her house and she would patiently listen to me try to sound the syllables out until it became too painful, and then she would offer to just read the book for me.

In Year 4, the teachers divided the children into learning groups of appropriate levels: 1 being the highest, reserved only for the smartest little fuckers, and 5 being the lowest for, you know, the challenged children. I assumed I wouldn't be in the higher groups – I knew I couldn't read and that my maths skills were ridiculous – but I was still really shocked when they put me in group 5.

My mum, who had to spend 70% of her full-time weekly wage on rent and was constantly in debt to her work's petty cash, got a tutor to come over and find out what was going on with me. The tutor taught me some things, like some random ways of remembering my nine times tables with my fingers, and she complimented my drawing, but that's pretty much all I retained. I was a very fast learner with the attention span of a shithouse goldfish.

In Year 5, while holidaying with my dad, he was advised to cut all of the preservatives out of my diet and see if my concentration improved. I remember being spoken about as if I wasn't there. To me, not being able to read or concentrate was just who I was; it didn't feel like it was that big a deal. Of course, nothing improved.

At the end of Year 6, my teacher made me stand up in front of the class and read her the answer to the two last questions of our social studies homework. When I didn't know them, she screamed, "Of course you don't! This whole class knows how dumb you are."

I wanted to die. Annaliese looked over at my burning red face, cringing, as if it had brought unthinkable pain even to her.

In Year 7, my best friend overheard my music teacher telling my teacher that I was talented. My teacher responded that I would fail: "Just watch, she always does." My torn best friend asked me if I wanted to know; of course I did.

In Year 8, at the age of twelve, I was asked to leave my high school for fighting with another student.

In Year 9, I was asked to leave my second high school, a Catholic school, for not wearing my hat or showing any signs of improving my grades. The older girls on my street told me they had voted that I would be the first girl to lose her virginity, the most likely to smoke and the first to drop out of school.

At fifteen, I started a course to pass Year 10 so I could go to TAFE. They taught us low-level skills; one teacher even instructed us how to push trolleys. Students dropped like flies from heroin overdoses. I nearly had a threesome with a girl who identified as a witch and her homeless mate, but thankfully chickened out at the last minute.

I thought of this school as the university of the dero. If you couldn't pass this course, one that doesn't actually require an IQ, you were in serious trouble.

And guess who couldn't pass it?

I just couldn't concentrate. In the end, I purchased a bottle of dextroamphetamine from some ADHD kid/businessman in the making, and what do you know? I passed with flying colours within three weeks. My teachers had no idea what had gotten into me. The truth is I was completely wired, and I developed a serious anxiety condition and insomnia for the first time in my life. So as fun as being a brain was I put the drugs away, took my certificate, and ran.

My boyfriend's mum told me that we were going in different directions; I didn't have a future and he was at uni. She told me that if I didn't find a way to catch up, he would leave me behind. But I had no path to travel, no doors to open. Despite my deep-down knowledge that I wasn't dumb, that I was someone, that I had a voice and a brain that was capable of understanding so much, I was quickly becoming what everyone expected me to become: nothing.

I never completed any TAFE courses, or returned to any type of education. I just wanted to get the fuck out of there.

MY BIG "FUCK YOU" MOMENT

Whenever anyone ever asks me why I became a hairdresser, I recall this one day I was walking down Brunswick Street in Melbourne, talking to my mum on the phone. She had always been so supportive of my sense of adventure, told me not to worry about being cautious and to just do it – travel, fall in love with rock stars, have fun – but this time was different. I was a waitress doing a few shifts a week, making just enough to buy cigarettes and pay rent, and my mum sounded worried.

She said, "Con, where are you going? Maybe you need to come home. It's time to sort out some kind of life. I worry so much."

I knew that while she would never say it, all that my mum wanted was a successful kid, kind of like flicking the finger to all of those fuckheads who doubted her unconventional ways. But I wasn't that child. I was nothing to write home about, unless you consider double-dropping ecstasy an achievement? I couldn't ease her mind, so I hung up the phone. I walked past a hairdressing salon with a sign on its window, *1st year apprentice wanted*, and the rest is history. I got some of the best hairdressing jobs in Melbourne. I wasn't even a particularly good hairdresser, but I understood shapes and colours, I made people laugh and I found my place with gay men. For the first time in my life I found men who loved me for me, who wanted nothing from me but a hilarious night out. They respected me, gave me a masculine warmth that I craved, and an equal give and take friendship.

Some time later, I was applying for *Big Brother* 2005 and was forced to use a computer. I was so frustrated that I had to use a fucking computer, but a large part of this round of auditions was writing and fuck, did I have some funny stories to write. I think I wrote a little essay about how much I hated my granddad, not so funny now that he's dead.

In the internet cafe, a friend showed me the registration number and told me to put it in. I couldn't and he was confused. I can't look at a number and read it out or copy it, but if you read it to me I can, so I covered the surrounding numbers, copying each number individually without the distraction of its surrounds.

My friend was very close to a psychologist, and he repeated this incident to the psychologist, who then chatted to me and told me that I had dyslexia and possible ADHD.

Who cares, right? School was done and dusted. I had no qualifications and kind of relied on the gift of the gab by now.

And out of the 25,000 people who auditioned for *Big Brother,* I was asked to be on the show. Sure, I know that doesn't make me special, but it makes me more than nothing… right? I was kicked out for being a young fuckhead, but I was still chosen and that meant everything.

I wrote. I travelled and wrote, fell in and out of love and wrote, painted and wrote, had babies and wrote. Sometimes blogs, sometimes short stories and sometimes just updating a status on Facebook. Writing was never about "literature", it was always about communication.

Every publishing company in the country rejected my writing, but still I wrote. When I was too tired, I'd write about how tired I was; when I was inspired, I'd try to inspire; and when I was down, I'd document it, for anyone and everyone. I lost the ability to be embarrassed by who I am. Sometimes my behaviour or actions still embarrass me, but I am no longer embarrassed about who I am.

When I was 28, I decided to find out if I could go to uni. I wanted to be a psychologist, to help people and, above all, I wanted to write.

I sat my STAT test to gain mature-age entry, convinced I would fail. Halfway through the test, I developed hives all over my body and tried to give up. But I didn't. I stayed. I had something to prove to everyone and, deep down, to myself.

A few months later, I received a letter in the mail stating that I was in the top 92% in the country for that year's intake. I could go to any university I wanted, and the best accepted my application.

That was my "fuck you" moment. To the teachers who hadn't believed in me, to the parents who hadn't believed. Fuck you, I still believed.

Of course, I didn't last. I had two kids and found it incredibly hard. I still had all of my original issues with conventional classroom studies. I couldn't even learn the online library logins or how to reference an essay.

So, I quit to live my life to my own beat. And I continued to write.

Which brings me to today. Best-selling author with a sold-out clothing line, her own radio show, over a million social media followers, and having personally funded two safe houses for abused children in Kenya.

The dumbest kid in the class? There's a "fuck you" moment right there.

Or is it? Did all of those people who ignored me and put me down just fuel me? Did they keep me humble? Is that the key to my success? Or is it luck? I really don't know.

My mum puts my success down to grit. She said that most people couldn't be fucked doing the things that I do, but I don't stop. Some nights, I'm up all night, painting or writing. I see things through to the very end. I suppose coming from a place of limited options, with hills that look too steep, I can't ignore any opportunities. I can't let anything pass me by.

One thing I know for sure, something my aunty told me when I was young, when I didn't believe a word of it: "Con, the hard things that happen to you, the things that you get through, are your biggest gift. They will be from where your success rises." I had no idea what she meant. How could that be true? Surely that is just something someone says…

But I look back on the last couple of years and I ask myself what my greatest stresses have been, and there are two. The first would have to be the stress of early parenthood, finding my feet, crying for days, anxiety, depression and confusion. Some days, I didn't know if I was going to get through it.

The second would be my weight, which sounds so superficial, but to anyone out there who has body image problems (is there anyone who doesn't?), you will understand the number of hours wasted on agonising and self-hatred over your fucking body and how you look.

Now, I know I have over a million followers and a radio show, but guess where my income comes from? The book I wrote on my struggles through early pregnancy, and the inclusive clothes designed for healthier body image. How's that for ironic? How could I possibly speak to that many women if I didn't know what they are going through, if I hadn't been there to the extreme? How could I design clothes that make women feel better about their bodies if I too didn't need to feel better about mine?

Like Buddhists who believe problems are like waves – one crashes and another forms – I remind myself every day that if today's worry worries me enough, maybe it will become my next success story. Because when you love something, it becomes a part of you, and you shouldn't stop, even if you can't spell!

This is why I don't employ someone to edit my blogs. This is why my spelling fuck-ups are there for the world to see, and I never get my "they're" and "their" correct, or my "women" and "woman"… and don't get me started on "you're" and "your".

This is why I celebrate my kids' academic achievements, but never worry about their failures.

This is why you will never embarrass me by calling me stupid.

I am who I am, and if there are any other "dumb" kids who can't spell, or read, or even learn how to use a fucking PC, I want them to see themselves in me, because there are so many different definitions of smart.

Nobody believed I could do it.

And I did it.

Conventional education isn't for everyone; the best we can do is hope that our kids come out of it knowing that there is a place for them, there is a path for them, they just need to create it.

Maybe it's not a jumbled brain in a clear world? Maybe you live in a jumbled world with a clear brain?

Don't let the world change your mind; let your mind change your world.

It's never too late to be who you were born to be.

SOMETIMES, THE END IS THE ONLY PLACE TO BEGIN

FLYING SOLO: STRENGTH, FEAR AND CENTRELINK

Nearly two years ago, I sat in my backyard with a cup of tea and asked myself, *if I were to kill myself, how would I do it?* It's one of the many bored thoughts that go through your mind when you haven't had any adult company in weeks and are sick of picking ingrown hairs out of your bikini line. But it is just an idle thought, not really a proposition. On becoming a single mum with four kids five years and under, I was giving myself a few minutes to envision what it would be like to just let everything go, to not wake up. I guess I was looking for the only real plausible escape that I could find.

I had been to Centrelink that day. I was claiming the single mum's pension as I was living in the house on my own, with the kids, and was finding it more relaxing than I had feared. To be frank, I was kind of excited to see how much cash I would be entitled to now I had added twins to my pack.

I lined up for over an hour, even though I knew apparently everything is done online now. If I was to try to sign into some automated system that wanted a password from six years ago, and then wanted to use an email address that I hadn't used in five years to confirm the reset of that password, my laptop would find itself in serious danger of being hurled against a wall. And it's hardly the laptop's fault.

So, after an hour in a line that you'd have better luck scoring meth in than actually sorting out a welfare payment, while a toothless woman with a longneck of beer entertained the kids for me, I was finally served.

"Constance Hall?" said a lady holding an iPad.

Her expression could only be summed up with: "What kind of bullshit is this dumb bitch gonna serve me?" as she faked a smile and asked me what the reason for my visit was.

"I'm here to apply for the single mother's pension," I responded, head held high.

"Ok, well that's all done online, go to this website…" she started, writing some government website on a post-it note for me, but I was having none of it. I hadn't sat next to a guy who stank of piss and drooled over my tits while my four kids screamed, for over an hour, only to be sent away.

I interrupted with, "I don't have the internet," and shot her a sassy look.

"That's fine, we have the internet here. You're welcome to get in line to use one of our computers for free." And shot me an even sassier look.

I was left with no choice but to pull out the big guns. "But I can't read."

We stared each other in the eye and she gave me a hint of a smile as she admitted defeat and let this sassy, lying bitch with no integrity through for her first meeting with a social worker.

The rest of it was actually pain-free. The chick I had the appointment with saw that I was at my breaking point, and halved the usual wait time for my payments to start. For the first time since having the twins, I was starting to feel like I was making steps towards independence.

Unfortunately, when you have six-month-old twins, a three-year-old and a five-year-old, being out of the house is even more exhausting than being in the house, so I went home to the sanctuary of my backyard and a cup of tea.

Scrolling through Facebook, I was wondering why Sarah Louise from high school deserves a husband who comes home from work and hugs her tightly after a day of missing her unbearably; how Jessica Meagre, a girl I met out one night, managed to highlight her naturally black hair to a cool, dusty white colour; and thinking that if I was to top myself, I'd do it with pills – you know, to get one last kick.

These were my thoughts. This was how my brain was working: it had lost its humour, it had lost its zest, and it had lost me.

I remembered a dream that I'd had growing up, one that I had completely given up on. It was a dream of falling in love.

*

Being raised by a single mum, I struggled with the realities. I saw my mum work and work and work. We had no options. We had no weekends away; she would borrow from petty cash to get us through the weekend and pay it back on Monday, only to be borrowing again on Friday. We moved from rental to rental, and when I was a typical selfish kid and complained about all the things my friends had, my mum's answer always was, "well, their mum isn't a single mum." Thus began my long-standing fear of single motherhood.

I blamed everything on the fact that I didn't have a normal family – the struggling, the boredom, the loneliness. When I envisaged what I was going to be when I grew up, kids never came into it. I was never that kid who dreamed of being a bride, or having a white picket fence. I dreamed about being a famous rock star and falling in love…

The last thing I wanted to be was a mum, and being a single mum was just never an option. I watched my mum struggle; we moved house all the time and were always running out of money. My mum's varied explanations of why I couldn't participate in what all the other kids were doing always included the words "single mum", and I developed an irrational fear of becoming a single mum myself.

After I had my first child I realised it was quite possible that, at some point, I was going to become a single mum. I needed the security of a job, and I needed the independence, so I went to work in a barbershop. The lousy pay barely even covered childcare, but I had to do it. Women's refuges, council flats and Centrelink lines were constantly hovering in my thoughts.

Having a baby is terrifying, and not everyone is lucky enough to have one with a man they trust. It can make things unbearable. You're at you most vulnerable: bloated, giving birth and shitting all over a hot doctor, painful boobs that just don't seem to do the trick, flat nipples, infected fannies, exhaustion and postnatal depression. When a woman has a baby and she isn't the main breadwinner, she can freak out. Birth, breastfeeding, the pay gap – so many things contribute to fears of "What's going to happen to me?" It can feel like your life is in someone else's hands. Many women are in unhealthy relationships, with a bloke that they can't trust, a bloke who ridicules them or tries to control them and doesn't support them at all. I have seen it, I have friends in these situations and I am written to by hundreds of women going through it.

You go into survival mode, and wonder how you're going to get through it at all. The fact is that we don't all fall in love with people who we would trust with our lives. What you need to see you through it is a rock; an emotionally available rock.

Pregnancy books never refer to women in abusive, controlling or neglectful relationships. They seem to all assume that everyone's living the Insta-perfect life. The truth is a large number of women are doing it, or have done it, tough.

Today, we do have resources to help, but all I hear when I hear the word "resources" is "waiting lists". What you really need is a support network and we don't all have them.

I have a friend whose husband cheated on her the day after she gave birth.

Another whose husband broke up with her the day of her scheduled C–section.

Another whose husband refused to buy her sanitary pads after the baby was born, saying it was a wasted expense and she could use washable flannels. Luckily I came over that day and showed her how much more convenient his folded-up boxer shorts were for the job. It made sense: flannels go on faces, boxers go on bums.

Women stay for so many reasons: for many it is hope, the hope that they would become a family again, the hope that there is still love there, and the hope that somehow happiness will prevail. In a dying marriage, you get snippets, little snippets of happiness.

At the age of 31, I was stuck. I had fucked my life up so thoroughly, I felt like everyone hated me. I hated me, and my pregnancy with the twins took my patience, so even my kids were hating me.

I had worked hard my whole life. I left school before even finishing Year 10 and started to work, sometimes two jobs at a time. Independence and adventure were everything to me, and I'd fucked myself out of ever having a chance with either again.

The babies took everything of me. I felt like I no longer existed. I was purely a vessel to give my kids life. Even my friends had given up on me, tired of me continually cancelling on them.

At the time, I took a lot of comfort in my single-mum friends. They all had their shit together and that inspired me. I remember one of my friends, Kristie, and I messaging each other into the late hours of the night while I was breastfeeding the twins, who never, ever slept.

I was my usual depressing self: *I swear I'll never meet anyone else. I'd been unlucky in love when I'd been single with no kids. I couldn't even pull a drug-addicted homeless guy now, I'm just gonna settle in for life on my own.*

Her response, with an overwhelming amount of conviction, was: *That's bullshit Con; you will find love. But you need to get strong first. And I promise happiness will come.*

And for some reason, not only did I believe her, I never forgot her words.

Within six months, everything would be different.

Within a year, I would be a completely different person, living a completely different life. Unbeknownst to me, I would have the hard times to thank for everything.

*

When becoming mums, women worry about so much: "Will I be able to breastfeed?" "What about cot death?" "How will I get my baby to sleep?" "Will I be a good role model?"

What we never worry about is one thing that should be at the top of our priorities: loneliness. This really strange thing happens to the women of the western world: they have a baby, everyone comes over for a whole week… and then you don't hear from them for a year.

Why? Not because your friends are cunts who don't care. People think you have enough company… as in your children.

Now, I don't know if anyone reading this has spent a whole day with my children but… they are not company. Company is laughing and drinking wine; company is stalking your ex-boyfriends on Facebook; company is a shoulder to cry on. Company is not watching *Peppa Pig* while stirring bolognese and making a doctor's appointment for your feral two-year-old son, whose dick is infected again because he is literally obsessed with it.

That's work.

For some reason, friends assume your brain and heart are filled up and you don't need them anymore.

Imagine you were at home for twelve hours on your own with no kids every day. Your mates would pop over every single day, just to see if you are OK. Because most of the time, you're not OK, you do need friends, new ones and old ones and everything in between. We call it a village, only most of us don't know what being part of a village feels like. The closest thing we have to a village is on online community noticeboard Facebook groups and I've often witnessed more diplomacy watching *National Geographic* document a mass animal slaughter.

I wrote this blog in 2017, after moving to Margaret River and realising I had made not one single friend in a year and was depending solely on my lover to fill me up:

The lack of a village has affected women in so many more ways than we know.

Especially when we have children.

Parenting babies has become one of the most isolating things we will ever embark on.

Our village has been replaced with four walls and an iPhone.

And I for one am lonely.

I moved to the country nearly a year ago, and partly because I am so busy with all of these kids, partly because I haven't put in enough effort, I still haven't found my village.

Women are isolated nowadays because we are expected to be self-sufficient; we don't need to go down to Penny's house to swap milk for tomatoes, we have childcare so we don't need to ask Alice to watch our kids while we go to the doctor, the street doesn't even know each other, let alone cook together. In fact, asking for help has become so far from the community norm that we now sound like we "aren't coping" if we reach out.

And guess what the silent cost of our lack of village is? Our relationships.

Because all the things we should be getting from our village, we expect from our relationship.

Our cups are empty and we need them filled, only society has structured us to only rely on one person. Our partner.

We are expected to be breadwinners, best friends, housekeepers, on each other's side in arguments with the in-laws, an ear, a shoulder, to work hard – but spend quality time with each other, no, take the kids out I need time alone, go to the shops, cook for me and for fuck's sake, be sexually adventurous.

If we could open our doors to the community, have company and help each other all day, our cup would be 80% full before we even reunited at the end of the day with our partners.

Women are social creatures, we need each other like we need food.

Children need relationships with adults who aren't their parents.

And relationships need a bit of fucking pressure taken off them.

It's true what they say – it really does take a village.

I'm starting today.

Con x

Somebody once told me that every single shit thing that has ever happened to you is a gift, a blessing, and that every time you fall over, you learn how to get up. You will not only never fall in that spot again, but you'll also be able to help up another woman who has fallen over in that spot. I never really understood; I seemed to fall all the time. I'm pretty good at brushing myself off but never has anything good ever come of it.

But on this day, my loneliness pushed me to do something, the one thing that would change things forever. I started a blog.

I had been blogging for over ten years, but this time I was starting a page on Facebook, thinking that I'd gain a few hundred followers and we could connect, bitch about parenting, lift each other up through some shitty times... ya know, all that stuff.

I'd had enough of just writing an article that yet another media outlet would ignore.

Had somebody told me that within a year and a half, I'd have over a million followers that loved and supported me, who I'd be sharing every detail of my life and love with, and I'd be sitting in London after a sold-out tour of back-to-back shows, with the love of my life, my kids and his two kids, and writing my second book? I would have taken another sip of my tea, laughed, and told you to lay off the crack pipe. Because that kind of shit just doesn't happen.

Pregnancy books don't prepare you for the loneliness. Prepare yourself for it. Gather your squad, put yourself out there, be vulnerable, join Facebook groups and request new friends like you tell your kids to do at school. Don't be embarrassed, the rest of us are stuck at home feeling like desperate losers too.

Centrelink ain't nothing to be ashamed of. Welfare is your right as a Queen. Do what you gotta do to get out, get free and get happy.

Don't buy from the dealers in the Centrelink lines; meth is never the answer folks.

The future is never, ever, anywhere near as scary as the past tries to make us believe.

Your hardest times bring you your biggest rewards. Not today, maybe not tomorrow, but one day you will be grateful for all the areas you are a true expert in – yourself. You are your only expert. Use that.

IT'S GOING TO BE OK, IT JUST IS

My house was covered in flour because Billie-Violet and I were making zucchini slice for dinner. I was breastfeeding Snow with one hand, because I'm a fucking magician, Rumi was lying on the floor crying because I'm a very bad magician and Arlo was storming through the house, chanting that he wasn't going to eat his dinner. Then my mum walked in. So grateful she turned up, I handed her Snow, turned around, went to bed and cried.

I had been strong for too long.

So many parts of what I called life were not normal. I should not be crying that much, I should not be so unhappy, I should not be alone all the time. But I had no one to blame but myself. I had fucked my life up so much. I just fell apart. It's what I needed to do to rebuild myself. My mum was worried, and my friends were worried.

Women leave marriages all the time. We see it from the outside, but we never see it from the inside; we never see the tears and the trying, the complete loss of oneself. But it's always there, a mother would give up everything for her kids: her career, her money, her freedom and eventually her happiness, because she is convinced that is what she should be doing. It's as if we need to sacrifice ourselves in order to be a good mother. We can't be anything else but a mother.

How did we come to this conclusion? Our mothers? The competitiveness of internet mothering? It's funny how by trying to be the best mum we can, we lose sight of one of the most important aspects of parenting – being a good example. Being an example of someone who is defined by their marital status or financial status or the fact that they have kids or not. Being a good example certainly entails an element of putting your own life first.

I see my family doing sweet fuck all because they know I'll pick up the slack. The only way they'll actually pick up some slack is if I outright disappear. And that's why I work, to disappear.

If I could sneak back in time, into that room, and tell me with my puffy face that everything was gonna be OK, I would. But of course, everyone tries to, and nobody listens. We need to learn it for ourselves.

Listening to people bitch about women in divorces is something I have always despised. I find so many women are silent in a divorce, while so many men are so loud, and the public or the friends seem to always side with the "poor" man.

I recently asked my therapist why this is, and she explained to me, "Whoever leaves the relationship with the most guilt, whoever knows they fucked up and can't let go, hasn't learnt the lessons that their relationship was there to teach them. And they will be talking and blaming… What do you hear when you hear the words, 'but it's not my fault'? You hear a child, an immature little kid. Often women are just done by the time they leave. They don't want to explain themselves, don't want to bitch or blame. After years and years of going around in circles, they just want to move on."

Marriages end for all kinds of reasons; my counsellor once told me that the only marriage that was irreparable was one with irresolvable differences. For example, say one person wanted to live in Melbourne and one wanted to stay in Perth, or if one person wanted to start stripping and slay cock for a living, while the other wanted to buff and polish their white picket fence. Everything else can be worked on: marital indiscretions, contempt, falling out of love – you just need to want to.

He told me that married people fall out of love all the time, but the trick is that they don't do it at the same time. I loved that advice. It's normal to fall in and out of love but still remain connected. I have felt that – falling out of love and believing that I would never fall back in love, only to be completely solid again a month later.

Stop blaming yourself for your situation. Just because fixing it is your responsibility it does not make it your fault that you got there.

Victim blaming has convinced women that being a victim is something to be ashamed of. You're allowed to be tired because nobody's helping you. You're allowed to be angry because your partner isn't supporting you. You're allowed to cry over your fuckwit brother eating your last Ferrero Rocher. It's not your fault; the world is full of cunts. Now wipe away your tears and take a deep breath, because you've got this.

The loudest divorcee isn't necessarily the victim. Some people can be very convincing that they have been wronged, while the other partner isn't smug, they are just happy to be free. As a friend, and Queen, it's not our job to judge or disbelieve. It's our job to support with gin and tonics and tell each other how hot we look.

It's OK to fall out of love. It's OK for your partner to fall out of love. You can both fall in and out of love and still make it work, with respect. That's the fairy tale.

WHY ARE MEN ADDICTED TO EVERYTHING BUT US?

My marriage counsellor told me, "Marriages end every day for so many reasons and one of the most common is addiction."

When we hear the word "addiction", we often think of heroin or crack, but she was referring to more boring though no less serious ones: work addiction, or sex addiction, or going out with mates and drinking beer – any behaviour to avoid confronting themselves and their problems.

Don't get me wrong, both men and women fall into the trap of addiction, but my experience with the friends I have, the parents I know through school, and after listening to advice from psychologists, is that it's affecting more men than women. One of the main reasons is because often the man becomes avoidant of and loses presence in a relationship. In fact, I read that it's one of the most common reasons women leave their partners: they become tired of waiting for their husbands to notice them. A lot of men are left feeling baffled, shocked, heartbroken and remorseful when the love of their life leaves them.

If an unhappy man goes out with his friends, he can quickly forget all his problems. The minute he comes home and sees his wife and kids, reality kicks in. He is reminded of the bills, the back fence he hasn't fixed in six months, and the time he hasn't put into his kids. So he distracts himself again, going into the office and catching up on some paperwork.

And how does this leave poor old wifey feeling? Like she is the problem, like she is a drainer, a nag, somebody worthy of nothing but avoidance.

I have watched so many good men fall apart, begging me to talk to their girlfriends or wives for them. These are the same men that I have watched ignore their hardworking partners for so many years. It breaks my heart. They are good men; they just couldn't see the forest for the trees before it was too late, and they lost everything.

I am so tired of hearing people defend avoidant men by saying, "but he is a hard worker, he provides for his family."

To make a marriage work, you need to do so much more than work hard. You should both be working hard, and both be providing for your family, but self-awareness is also so important.

If you lack insight into your relationship and you're not bothering to put everything into it that it needs to succeed, whether that's counselling, date nights or just half an hour chatting before bed, then bring home as much bacon as you want, coz it's never gonna be enough.

*

I am not avoidant. I confront the relationship, its problems and its beauty almost obsessively, even when I know the best thing for me to do would be to drop it and let go. But I can't. I want to get to the bottom of it. And I can spoil things by doing so.

But every man I've ever been with is avoidant. They avoid problems because they don't know how else to deal with them.

Meanwhile, a co-dependant like me reads that behaviour as "I don't care", when it really doesn't mean that at all.

Avoidant people find so many ways to avoid: going to sleep on a fight, leaving on a fight, drinking or taking drugs or becoming obsessed with work. And those are pretty much all the things my mates and I bitch about when we get together.

I wrote this blog after an informative chat with my psychologist:

One day at my psychologist, she mentioned to me that she sees a lot of men in her office. I asked why, and she responded that a lot of women are leaving men and they aren't coping.

Interesting.

So I asked, why are women leaving men?

She responded because heaps of men aren't present in the relationship and a lot of women are feeling lonely in their own homes.

That resonated with me, at the time I was feeling very lonely in my own home.

That very same day, I went to my local cafe and saw an old friend, a pretty tough "ladsy" kind of bloke, and he broke down right in front of me.

"She left me, I've tried everything, she won't take me back, I don't know what to do and I'm lost Con."

Two days later, I received a phone call from a family member who was suffering a breakdown after his wife had left him, he had even been hospitalised.

"What's going on?" I thought.

So at my following appointment with my psych, I picked the conversation up again.

"Why aren't men being present in marriages? Women warn them so many times before they leave, why can't they just pay attention?"

She responded with, "Because men, just like women, are suffering. Depression is rife, yet instead of reaching out and getting help they are distracting themselves. You see when someone isn't happy their family reflects that, just like when you are happy, the people who are the most intimate to you are like a mirror and they reflect how you feel. So if you are depressed, being home and present reflects that depression, so a lot of men become avoidant.

"Avoidant people do everything in their power to distract themselves, they go out a lot, they take on too much work, they drink too much, avoidant men will do anything to distract themselves from being here and being present."

"So, when the daily grind is getting blokes down, instead of saying, 'I'm down, help me out, mofos', they are pulling back and avoiding us like the plague, becoming less present to everything and then we get so lonely that we leave them and then they have pretty serious breakdowns?"

"Pretty much, Con."

A lot of men I know need to get a grip on this. I know they love their wives and I know their wives love them, but all will be lost if we can't find presence in the marriage.

I spoke to men I knew about this, and they told me that sometimes the pressures of keeping a roof over the heads and food on the table for a family is overwhelming. I'm trying to remember that more and more.

Relationships need patience, kindness and compassion.

Con x

Avoidant people will become addicted to anything that distracts them from... them.

Don't make the mistake of blaming yourself when your significant other avoids your family. They are avoiding themselves.

You can't change anyone. Only they can fix this. You can only change you, your reactions and responses.

Prioritise you, your strength. Find another hobby, change your career, take your existing hobby to another level. Ask yourself who you even are. Look back at your life... when were you most happy? Was it creating? Gardening? Studying? Watching porn? Who are you, independent of motherhood and wife life?

HOME

When I published *Like A Queen*, I was earning money for the first time since having the twins. People always think "famous" people are rich, but even though articles were being written about me nonstop, I was being stopped for photos everywhere I went and I even had people come to my house having heard that this is where I lived, I didn't earn a cent.

My website cost more to run than I received from advertising, so when I released pre-order sales of my book and some money started to come in, I knew things were going to change.

I was still miserable. I had always hated the suburb I lived in, the house was too small and the whole environment contributed to my depression. Suburban life doesn't suit me. Before I moved to Hamilton Hill, I had been in central Melbourne for years, having returned from living in London and Spain. It was never supposed to be permanent, and the more permanent it felt, the more corroded my soul felt. I tried everything to find a way to move. I would have been happy renting somewhere closer to the water or near a friend. I felt so isolated and unable to make the changes I knew I needed to make. I felt so isolated and trapped, I knew what I needed to do to be happy but didn't have the resources or the balls to make the changes.

The first thing I decided when I started to earn money was that I was going to move out. I couldn't stay in that brown, dry suburb any longer. I wanted forest or beach, anything but that. That house was killing me. I began house hunting immediately.

Like A Queen was buying me freedom.

I didn't know what to do with this sort of money. All I knew was that I wasn't going to be one of those idiots who ends up losing everything, doesn't have enough money for tax and goes bankrupt. I was being a total scrooge with it, not spending a cent, saving it all for a new house. I house-hunted in Fremantle, a place where you will pay a million dollars for a tiny house. I even put an offer on a house without getting pre-approval for a loan. Of course I didn't get it, because I definitely wasn't doing *that* well.

But something didn't feel right. Something was stopping me from jumping in full-force, from making it happen, which is so not me. I'm known for making shit happen. When I want something, I go for it and make it mine. I had no idea that my destiny was waiting for me, and it wasn't in Fremantle.

Every spare weekend I had, I would go "down south". I loved Margaret River passionately; loved the river, the forest, the beaches. My brother already lived there in my stepdad's house and, being a real-estate creep, I'd always have a cheeky look.

The minute I walked into my house I knew – this was it. It was half the price of anything I had been looking at in Fremantle, which meant that I could buy it, be mortgage-free and still have enough money for my tax bill. This purchase would leave me with nothing, but I didn't care. I was meant to live in this house.

It's surrounded by the tallest trees you'll ever see, has grapevines dripping around the deck, and the kitchen opens onto big garden beds, so if I was to ever cook, I could reach over and grab fresh herbs (that don't actually exist, because gardening, like cooking, isn't my thing).

It was perfect. I bought it. And for the first time since I embarked on this crazy life of blogging and writing books and being recognised everywhere I went, I sat down, took a huge deep breath and felt immensely proud of myself.

The universe will give you subtle hints, hinting where you need to go, a little nudge in the right direction. If you don't pick up on the hints it will trip you over. If you get up and keep walking in the same direction, it will shoot you in the leg until you finally turn around. Easiest is the life that hears the hints.

WHEN WOMEN KICK THE BIGGEST GOALS BUT NEVER WIN THE GAME

I couldn't go to the supermarket in less than half an hour as I'd get stopped so many times – selfies, life stories – I loved it all. It was kind, it was women, it was a sisterhood that I had been missing, it was "us" against "them" and our army was growing. We were fighting loneliness, sexism, postnatal depression and body issues, with love, kindness and humour.

What could go wrong?

My blog grew and grew, but sooner or later my life would change. I once blogged about my life, but now my life was about my blog.

I wanted to be honest in my blog and blog about everything that was really happening, but I often received negative feedback for sharing anything negative – totally ironic when you have a page that's famous for its honesty. Nobody wants to hear the bad stuff. Apparently, you can share anything you want on Facebook as long as it's totally honest… but you can never share anything heavy. But, honestly? Life gets heavy. Only when you share it, you're "oversharing".

One lady wrote a comment: *No wonder nobody loves you, with the amount of oversharing you do. Nothing is personal.*

If only she knew how much I was keeping inside and how little I was sharing.

Two years ago, the world fell in love with me; last year, they wanted to rip me to shreds. I understand, I get it, but I don't know if I am built for it. I became Australia's most hated woman, and the only control I had was to turn off the internet.

My family and friends couldn't believe it. They tried to defend me and frantically called to see what they could do. I told them I didn't want to know about it. If this is what I go down for – pursuing happiness – let it be.

When Brad Pitt and Angelina Jolie broke up, she was the villain. He received standing ovations while presenting awards and it was predicted that she would never work again. When Brad was accused of getting violent with the children, Angelina was blamed for keeping the kids from him. He was the one in a relationship when they met, but she's the homewrecker. She has donated millions of dollars of her own money to her humanitarian work and is still portrayed as the evil mastermind. In divorce, women are the villains. When you say anything to defend yourself, you are either oversharing or tearing someone down. You're supposed to wait in silence.

This blog I wrote after a dinner party with friends, a simple conversation that we hear all the time, yet this time it fell on different ears; it fell on ears that had had enough of the inequality that we face in divorce. I was surprised to turn my phone back on and see that it had gained over a hundred thousand likes. Seems I'm not the only woman who's done with it.

At a party a few weeks ago, listening in on a conversation about *Jenny* (the chick who's loving her life after resurrecting from a shit divorce):

Me: What's she done?

Girl 1: Well ever since she split up with *Darren* she's been a really shit mum, she gets babysitters most weekends and goes out a lot.

Girl 2: And she's already introduced her kids to her new boyfriend, which must be so confusing for them.

Girl 1: I deleted her off Facebook, I don't want to know about it.

Me: What does Darren think?

Girl 3: I don't think he knows. When he left Jenny for that other chick, he moved over to Queensland but he pays child support... like every week.

Me: Right... Did you delete him off Facebook?

Girl 1: No, I didn't want to get involved.

Me: Right.

So just to recap, in the same year that Jenny gets dumped by her husband for another woman, she also loses her friends because they don't think she handled her whole world being turned upside down the way that she was "supposed" to, and despite working full time to support them, living for them, doing everything in her power to keep them secure and loved, getting a babysitter on the weekend and a new boyfriend makes her a shit mum.

Darren on the other hand, who dumped his wifey for another woman, ran away from his kids and is probably drinking cocktails by a pool somewhere with some weird-as-fuck new midlife crisis hairstyle, is still "good" because he slings them $170 a week... without fail...

Fact: I don't hate Darren. I don't know the full story and I have made some pretty bad decisions myself in my time too. I am simply pointing out that if Jenny did what Darren did, she would have no friends and be outcast from society.

Fact: Jenny's kids are fine. I called her up and went to see them all. They rock, they think babysitters once a week, or fortnight, are totally exciting, and they love her new boyfriend, who barely comes over because Jenny is too busy basically winning at life as a single mum.

Fact: A divorce is the time that Queens need each other the most. Sadly, I hear too many Queens talking about how they lost a lot of their friends during their divorces.

Be forgiving. Be supportive. Be Queens.

Con x

There was, and is, still so much that I wanted to say but I didn't and I won't. I got through that time by only writing fun blogs, by writing a bit more social commentary, and a little less about relationships and my life.

I look now back at what I have written, in my blogs and first book, and I can't help but notice one major thing: I was normalising unhappiness, and my misery was validating everyone else's. I got so many messages from people who were in terrible situations, telling me that I made them realise it was OK, because I saw the humour and made it funny, so they could too.

I believe it is hugely therapeutic to share your problems with each other – it helps you feel less alone – but I hope I never made anyone accept unhappiness and stop striving for a happier, or more free, life. Turning misery into humour was one thing, expecting people to still love you when you are pursuing happiness is another thing completely.

I had come along at the right time and been a breath of fresh air for anyone suffering, for anyone who was fed up with Instagram mums and their perfect lives, and needed to feel normal. Nobody wanted that to change. Nobody was interested in my pursuit of happiness.

There is a saying: you learn who your true friends are when you are in need. Unfortunately, sometimes with women, it's not always about being in need. We are there for each other in times of need, we help each other when one is struggling, but I honestly believe you often learn who your true friends are when times are good. When you're ecstatically happy, who's still there? Who's celebrating your wins? And who's fucked off to bitch about you behind your back? Who's seething in jealousy and trying to drag you down?

I experienced this when I finally started putting myself first, making myself happy, and when I fell in love. I wasn't so loveable anymore. My haters came out in full force. Everyone had a different reason to hate me – I wasn't putting my kids first, or I hadn't conducted myself the way society expects women to behave. I had seen it before, so many times. Friends would separate, everyone would be happy because they didn't like the way he treated her. She would move on and all of a sudden she's the talk of the town. She no longer "walks" down the street, instead she "struts". She has her children six days a week and is accused of negligence for getting a babysitter on one of those nights, whereas her ex has them one night a week and is hailed a hero for doing the "righty".

Comparison is the enemy of the sisterhood.

It's not fair and we would be so much stronger if we could just stick together. Men seem to have each other's backs in a divorce, you never hear a man saying:

Bloody Bob, he lost Sharon. I warned him, keep going out all the time and she'll walk. Good on Shaz for leaving and making a happier life for herself.

No, you hear:

Poor Bob. Mate, all he did was try and support that family. We all need to go out on the weekends and blow off some steam, it was harmless. Now Sharon's destroyed his whole life.

But women? We seem to judge each other when we should be supportive. And do you know why? Because we can't help but compare ourselves to Sharon:

How did Sharon get the strength to walk?

Or:

How come Sharon didn't have to stay and put up with a husband who works all week, goes out on the weekend and sleeps in between?

It forces us to make excuses, excuses that make us feel better about the things we are coping with, yet haven't changed:

Well, I could have left too if I didn't give a shit about my kids and their relationship with their father.

Or:

I hear she left him for someone else, who could do that to the father of their kids?

And bam! We don't have to compare ourselves to Sharon anymore, because she is a bad person and your unhappiness is due to the fact that you're a good one.

Why should we judge Sharon at all? Why do we need to judge any woman? It only leads to false assumptions and trust me, I'm no saint, I have done my fair share of judging too.

There was this woman at school pick-up every day.

I don't know what it was about her. She drove a nice car, held her head high and always had a blowdry.

She spoke in a posh accent, wore nice (non-stained) clothes and barely ever spoke to me.

There I was, with my tits out, breastfeeding my babies, smelling like dried milk with matted hair, a puffy face from a morning in tears, no shoes and a partial bogan accent.

It was like she was put on this earth to amplify my insecurities.

So I did what a lot of women do and I tried to instigate a "chat" about her with another mum, partly out of intrigue and partly hoping to make my feral self feel better.

But this other mum's advice hit me with a big reality check.

"Talk to the woman, not about her"

So, one day I decided to talk to her.

I sat next to her on the brick retaining wall outside the kindy room. I found out she is an ex-addict and holds AA meetings to help out other addicted women that want sobriety. I found out she struggles with her marriage, her kids and her health just like the rest of us. I found out that she is a million things, snobby not being one of them.

She is one of the most inspiring women I know.

Turns out I have a confident exterior too. Turns out that while sitting there, hating my life without the confidence to talk to these gorgeous mums, they didn't have the confidence to talk to me. They thought I was too free, too relaxed and that I thought I was too cool.

And that mum is now one of my best friends; we bitch about our men together, our kids and we laugh all the time.

So now that I'm at a new school, I know that a lot of folks have their opinions on me these days and unfortunately a lot of the gossip has gotten back to me, I'd like to remind mums everywhere to *talk to the woman, not about her.*

Con x

Bringing the sisterhood back and recreating a village starts with one small thing: changing our language around how we speak about fellow Queens. We are all pretty good at speaking to each other but it's time to start speaking about each other in a positive light.

Support women in divorce. You don't know the full story and it's got absolutely nothing to do with yours.

Don't put up with pain, as before long it becomes normal. You would be surprised at the levels of agony people live with because it has been normalised.

Other women's misery will not lead to your happiness, and other women's happiness is not going to steal yours. As a collective we have been freed of repression, but are still caged by the residual judgements and jealousy caused by our fear that there is not enough freedom and happiness for us all. There is enough for us all, and this key will unlock us together as a team – the Queen team.

Start small. Say one kind thing about another woman every day, to her and to someone else. Then move to actively supporting someone once a week. Pick her kid up from school or just invite someone to coffee. Let your sisterhood grow like wildfire.

DO THE MOTHERFUCKING DISHES

Sitting in my garden, rewarding myself with a cup of tea after washing my sixth load of clothes for the day, making school lunches for the following day, preparing for dinner and cleaning the kitchen while Denim had a nap because he was tired after surfing, I smashed out this piece of writing with such anger I needed a screen protector on my phone.

Recently while bitching about the fact that I do absolutely everything around my house with a bunch of friends all singing "Preach Queen" a friend said to me, "If you want help you need to be specific... ask for it. People need lists, they aren't mind readers."

So I tried asking... specifically,

"Can you take the bin out?"

"Can you get up with the kids? I'm just a little tired after doing it on my own for 329 years."

"Can you go to Woolies? I've done three loads of washing and made brekkie, lunch, picked up all the kids' school books, and dealt with the floating shit in the pond."

And yeah, she was right... shit got done.

But I was exhausted, just keeping the balls in the air... trying to remember what I had to ask to be done, the constant nagging...

And do you know what happened the minute I stopped asking...?

NOTHING.

Again.

And so I've come to the conclusion that it's not your job to ask for help, it's not my job to write fucking lists. We have enough goddamn jobs, and teaching someone how to consider me, and my ridiculous workload, is not one of them.

Just do it.

Just think about each other. What it takes to run the goddamn house. Is one of you working while the other puts up their feet?

Is one of you hanging out with mates, while the other peels the 30th piece of fruit for the day?

Is one of you carrying the all the household weight?

Because when the nagging stops, when the asking dies down, when there are no more lists...

All you're left with is silent resentment. And that, my friends, is relationship cancer...

It's not up to anyone else to teach you consideration. That's your job.

Just do the fucking dishes without being asked once in a while, motherfuckers.

Con X

Anybody that's ever had a child enter the kitchen and ask if they can "help" understands full well that when someone isn't helping properly, they aren't any help at all.

The mental load is real and it's exhausting. What makes me the manager of the house? What makes it OK for my partner to go from his Mumma's nest to mine?

I realised there were some severe inequality issues the moment I squeezed out my spawn.

Why do all of my friends ask permission to leave the house without their child, while their spouses can pop down to the shop, go and check out Troy's new car, have a beer on the way home? Without ever asking you…

Even me today: "Denim, I'm going out for a drink with my brother. I've made dinner, I've done the washing and the twins are bathed and they've peed. They just need to be put into bed. Cool?"

I still struggle with feeling like it's my right to just say, "I'm popping out" without it becoming a "prepper" for one of the thousands of natural disasters we have.

Now we could spend a lifetime nagging and begging men to change, to step up, to do it because they love us… only to get called a nag: "I said I'll do it, you don't have to ask me 700 times."

Do you know what? The majority of these men have grown up with every single one of their needs met… by a woman. And what makes it worse? So have we.

It's rare to find a man whose dad cooked for him, picked him up from school or did the washing.

So what are we left with today? A world that's changing, a world where women, praise the lord, are expected to work, where men and women are heading towards equality and really, really trying.

Only when we fought for equality, I don't think this is exactly what we meant. An 18% pay gap and 30% more working hours than our equals, our brothers and husbands… I don't think we were marching and burning our bras because we were bored and wanted more stuff to do…

Peace, generosity, love and equality all start at home.

I asked my cousin, a clinical psychologist, one day, "What's with men, why can't we change them? We have changed laws and wages and child care benefits, why can't we change men in the home?"

And she responded, "Because changing behaviour is the easy part. You can change anyone's behaviour, threaten them, bribe them, beg them, it's all pretty easy. Changing someone's belief system is a whole other story. If someone fundamentally believes something is not 'his job', he may be able to do it because you asked him to do it, but he won't be able to keep it up."

Light bulb.

Of course you can't. If some far-right extremist sat me down for weeks and weeks pleading with me to understand that same-sex marriage is wrong, I wouldn't change. I couldn't change. I was raised to believe in marriage equality… I know it's right. No matter how many times my partner gets mad about my dirty undies on the floor, I don't change. Why? Because I know it doesn't matter.

So what can we do?

Don't look at me. I'm not the fucking man whisperer. I'm in love with a man who would be literally dead if he did any less around the house.

But I know this.

It's our responsibility to raise children with different belief systems. And that means they need to witness you putting you first. Even if your belief system tells you it's wrong, slams you with a tsunami of parental guilt, ignore it. Make your children witness Mum going to work, Mum going out with friends, Mum painting her toenails sipping a Kahlua, while Dad serves dinner, and Dad has to pop two Xanax in the mornings to find the school fucking uniform that couldn't possibly have disappeared again…

Because if you want your daughters and sons to grow up in a world different to this one, one where the changes aren't just talked about but are actually implemented, then they are gonna need to see *you doing your thing, Queen.*

I'm not saying that all men are lazy sacks of shit…

Juggling too many balls and carrying too heavy a mental load will lead to a) a nervous breakdown or b) a change in sexuality.

Putting yourself first is not just for you, it is for the greater good of woman- and mankind.

Never forget that parental guilt is not there to tell you you're a shit mum. Shit mums don't have parental guilt. Parental guilt reminds you that you're a great mum who loves, feels and takes too much on.

IT'S ALL ABOUT ME

LOVE

I have always been obsessed with love. I like to think I know everything there is to know about love. I don't pretend to have been blessed with any skills in the act of love, but when it comes to knowledge, I am your girl.

You can name any one of my friend's relationships and I will recite a romantic thing that one of them has said about the other. After half an hour of meeting me, I will have extracted this information out of you and stored it. I file away even tiny compliments, like when I cut a handsome older man's hair and told him that he looked very nice, and he replied, "Well, I had better, my wife is so beautiful I need to keep up."

Or my high school friend, who is coming up to her twentieth anniversary with her high school sweetheart, who told me, "He is now my life companion, closer than a husband, closer than a brother. He is just half of me now."

Or the tradie who was building my deck and I asked him if he ever fights with his girlfriend and received the response, "She suffers from anxiety, especially when we fight and I know what topics upset her, so I avoid them." I could always find something to love about everyone I met. Even if they weren't for me, I'd find something lovable about them for a friend.

When I fell pregnant with the twins, I was in the worst place I could imagine being. I was miserable, depressed and confused.

I had no idea why life threw me that card. I have always believed in a greater power, a reason for things, a need to pick up on signs in order to keep on track with your true path.

I remember once hearing Oprah say something along the lines of: "There are no mistakes. You can take detours in your life and feel life nudging you back to your path. When you don't feel right or things keep getting you down, you know you're on a detour, but you will always end up back on the path that you were meant to be on."

I came to the conclusion that I wasn't designed for great love. I was a very lucky kid; I had a dad who loved me and showed his love more than anyone else's dad.

I often think about the blokes who came before. Women are often expected to wipe their slate clean when they are with a new man, pretend that their past never happened. It's funny because my past made me who I am, the unlovable things I did moulded me into the lovable woman that I am today.

Love is why we are here. Never give up on the love you deserve.

GYPSY HEARTS

"Some people were put on this earth to create music, some to create visual art, others to make billions of dollars and some were put here with bleeding hearts whose sole purpose is to help others."

Javier's huge brown eyes and thick Spanish lips looked extra dewy at this small hipster cafe down an alleyway in Perth. He was wearing a scarf, ripped jeans and a knitted jumper, a European fish-out-of-water in the most isolated city in Australia, possibly the world.

"And you?" I responded. "What were you put on this earth to do?"

"Well, I…" a massive grin appeared on that gorgeous face of his, "I was put here to kiss your pussy."

I rolled my eyes, the type of eyeroll that's accompanied by a smile which suggests I more than tolerated his arrogance. Javier had broken my heart twice; I wasn't going to let it happen again.

I met him when I was 22, my first night working at a bar in St Kilda. I was collecting glasses on the dance floor on a night called "Double O", where different local musicians get together to play at different venues on the first Friday of every month.

I had just moved back from Melbourne and was sleeping on the shabby old couch of my dad's rental. I had applied for every bar and waitressing job I had come across in the paper.

I had applied for a few hairdressing jobs but that was a far-off dream; all the salons wanted a clientele list, I didn't even own scissors.

I had no boyfriend, no friends and no savings. I'd been moving between Melbourne and Perth for months, trying to establish myself somewhere, trying to figure out where was home. I was torn between the friends and social life I had in Melbourne and the sun and beach in Perth. Thus far, long-term, the beach usually wins for me, but for now, the cold streets of Melbourne felt the warmest.

I'd like to say I was lost, but that would imply that it was a temporary problem. Staying in my mum's house… temporarily; my sister's bed… temporarily; my nanna's couch… temporarily. And so on, and so on. I wasn't happy unless I was on the go and I excused this lack of responsibility with having a "gypsy heart". In other words, I was permanently lost. But I kind of liked it.

On this night, collecting glasses in the bar, trying to keep myself as busy as possible, I walked past him and our eyes locked. He had long, thick hair, huge brown eyes, thick lips and growth on his face. He was possibly the best-looking guy I had ever seen. I walked straight past him, neither of us taking our eyes off each other.

I looked back and saw that he had done a complete 180, and was following me, so I walked behind the bar, grabbed a cloth and pretended I was busy. He stood there, staring, confident enough to not give a fuck that he looked like a stalker.

Finally, I asked him if he wanted a drink and he said, "No, I want you."

After a couple of hours of playing hard to get, I finally gave him my number. Later that night, I was drinking my free staff beer after work, pretending to be really interested in what my new co-workers had to say, when I saw Javier. He was knocking on the window, motioning for me to let him in. I pretended I didn't see him; my new boss had a flirty vibe and he'd mentioned that I only got the job because I was pretty.

And I was, to give credit where it's due. The whole time I had been job hunting, while staying at my dad's house, I made it my mission to get fit and tanned. I was at my thinnest, my hair was at its longest, a golden brown on the ends from faded colour that I could not afford to touch up, but was totally working for me, and I was rocking a gorgeous tan. I knew that I needed to look a certain way if I wanted to get a job in hospitality, a sad truth that I had learnt years ago in my first bar job.

So when Javier wanted my attention, I refused to give it to him. I was aiming for full-time shifts instead of the two a week I'd been given, and the way to go about it wasn't to let the dickfuck who owned the place know I was already giving my number to customers instead of worshipping him.

The next night, I let Javier take me out for dinner. I was mesmerised by his accent, the years he had spent travelling in South America, the ten years he had just finished travelling all over Asia. He was a filmmaker and a piano player and worked as a barista to pay the rent. Like a good Spanish man, he knew how to talk to women and respect women, and making a woman happy was his number-one goal. And he made me so happy.

Javier has a cheekiness to him, he gets away with more than most would, he pays attention to you and makes you feel beautiful, but he also has a conservative side. He told me that I had had enough to drink one night, at a point in the night that I was really starting to have fun. I kind of felt like possibly it was a cultural difference, like European chicks know when to stop drinking, they never drink to get drunk, and Aussie chicks like to smash jugs and root surfers on the beach. Being told I'd had enough to drink made me feel a little misunderstood.

I spent hours letting him play piano for me. I cut his hair, we talked about Spain, he told me that I was the most beautiful girl he had ever seen, he met my dad and we laughed about everything.

I met his mates at the hostel, and I privately named our children the most exotic Spanish names. We fucked and fucked and fucked. He would totally lose control of his desire and say things and do things that gave me goosebumps for days just thinking about them. I was on cloud nine. I had no car and would walk everywhere and all of a sudden I'd see butterflies landing on flowers in front of me and, like a fuckhead, I'd literally start to skip and I knew, I knew that I was in the right place at the right time. His plans were to move to London and even though it had only been a short time since we had been together, we decided I would come and see him there.

And then, he was gone.

A friend of his back in Spain was going on holidays for a couple of months and asked Javier to run his restaurant for him. Free rent came with the job. Javier was a sucker for free rent and with guaranteed work, he had to leave… without much notice. He spent his last night at my dad's house with me. He picked up an old, out-of-tune guitar and played the saddest and sweetest tune before looking at the time and saying he had to go.

I caught the bus with him into the city and we stood on the street in each other's arms. He kissed me on the lips and on the forehead, wiped my tears and asked me not to cry.

Then he said words that I never forgot: "Come to London, but don't come for me. Come because you want to see London, come for you."

Translation: "I don't really love you. This was fun but you're clingy, blah blah blah, rejection, you're desperate and fat, blah, blah…"

I went home to lick my wounds. I recognised rejection before someone's mouth even opened. I have been rejected so much that I don't even know if it's rejection anymore. Like when you're scared of ghosts and they are all you ever think about, so you start hearing ghosts in the hallway and you don't know what's real anymore. I'll be talking to a guy at a bar and he'll only buy himself a drink and I'll consider it rejection and walk away.

I was once rejected by two guys in thirty minutes: one sent me a text message saying that I really needed to stop messaging him because we weren't even really together. And twenty minutes later another guy that I was seeing called me to tell me that his grandmother had died so we couldn't see each other anymore.

Ironically, this was the time in my life that I both looked my hottest and was rejected the most. How strange, considering that for my whole life I had a fundamental belief that if I just lost five kilos, grew my hair and got a tan, everything would be OK. Every time a guy rejected me, I'd think about how sorry that fucker's gonna be when I lose five kilos and get a tan…

That belief system got so bad that I was actually called "tanorexic" at one point and kicked out of the solarium for "overuse". The owner told me I'd look fifty at thirty if I continued and that I wasn't allowed back. Even the solarium rejected me.

And now I have to have my skin checked every six months because I fucked myself up so badly. The paranoia of skin cancer has become so bad that the last time I went to get my skin looked at, they kicked me out because it had only been two months since my last visit and they are worried I might be getting obsessive. Fucking great.

Someone once told me that when a woman sleeps with a man, she gains an extra 50% attraction to him, yet when a man sleeps with a woman, he loses 50% attraction to her. Which I'm sure is where the theory of holding out for as long as you can with a guy comes from. The longer that you hold out, the more he will want you, but the better you get to know him, the less you will want him. So when you guys finally bang, the scales will even out a bit and you could make for a successful relationship.

I was never one to hold out.

Headscarves, guitars, butterflies, passion, rejection and tears. Young hearts have so much to go through and only the lucky ones learn the true meaning of love.

GETTING SOME BRIT INTO YA

Looking smoking hot, I wasn't about to let rejection from Javier ruin my plans; I was saving money to go to London despite not exactly being invited. As a parting gift, Javier gave me his job at the restaurant. Some days I would do a double shift and then go and work all night at the bar, saving all the money I had and still managing to get shitfaced on Saturday nights, stumbling home to my couch at my dad's.

I'd knock over one of the cups of water he'd been using to rinse his paintbrushes, "Fucking shit!"

My dad would scream, "Shut up Con!"

And I'd lie down on some vintage couch that Dad found on the side of the road, and pass out to the comforting residual smell of the joint he'd smoked that evening while painting.

It was worth it. I had saved up nearly $10k and was well and truly on my way when I met Jules. Jules was a Jamaican British man with long black dreadlocks who was in fact "black" but didn't look it. His parents were Jamaican English and they looked full blown black, as did his brothers and sister. But Jules was a weird throwback whose skin was almost as pale as mine. It kind of turned into a party trick, half way through the night he'd pull out photos of his family and shock everyone that he was in fact black. Jules was just as fun as me and loved nothing more than to party. We partied hard. He lived in a share house full of dirty towels, mouldy food, cute boys and a gross old spa that you could probably get pregnant just sitting in. I should know; I fucked Jules in it. It was a brief encounter, full of fun times and too much booze.

When he asked me how the hell I was still single, I replied, "Because I have a Spanish boyfriend, I've kind of been doing the long-distance thing." It was clearly a lie; there was absolutely no reason for me to believe that I was in any kind of committed relationship with good old Javier, who never responded to my emails.

Jules was returning to England that January and I was planning to go that English summer. He tried to convince me to go with him for a holiday, instead of waiting until June and going indefinitely. It was a tough decision because he was so fun, but I had a vision. I was going to wear gypsy headscarfs and long skirts and go where the wind took me – Spain, France – meeting backpackers, living my life to the fullest. A holiday in England didn't really suit the theme I was going for. I wanted to be wild, free to draw on the sand by the Mediterranean. Jules understood; being from England, the arse-end of the wild west of this huge country was his version of freedom.

However, Jules, glorious Jules, gave me two presents that would change my mind. All that fucking in the pool wasn't without its consequences. One day while working at the restaurant I went to the toilet and I was pissing razor blades: two drips and a fanny of fire. I came out of the toilet and told the whole restaurant that I had a fucking bladder infection and had to go to the doctor. My boss shook his head.

"What?" I snapped.

"Well, let's just hope that's all it is. You are the most sexually active person here," he responded.

"What the actual fuck is that supposed to mean? Like, because I have had more than one boyfriend this year (this month), I must have an STD?"

He just looked away.

I had an STD. It was chlamydia. Yay!!! Thanks, Jules!

You can't get angry at someone for giving you an STD. You can't think they're dirty or an infected slut, because now you're dirty and infected, and you became infected in the exact same way they did, by being a dirty infected slut. I swear, there can't be many people who haven't ticked the chlamydia list in their past.

I went home, slapped him on the back of the head and handed him his pills. My doctor was kind enough to give me a repeat prescription because Jules had no Medicare card. His flatmates reminded him that he was a dirty infected slut, until they got tested and realised that cesspit pool parties have their own prices to pay.

Jules and I continued our love affair. He smoked loads of spliffs, I smoked loads of rollies, and we both drank loads of beer. It was what it was, no deep love but a comfortable one, and a love that I needed after having my heart stomped on by my Latino lover. That is, until the old due date of my period reared its ugly head and I was once again reminded that my irresponsibility had consequences.

I was at work and I couldn't think of anything but that, so I went to the chemist and I bought a pregnancy test. If I were reimbursed all the money I have spent on pregnancy tests, I'd be a rich woman. I went to the public toilets. I don't know why but I always do pregnancy tests in public toilets. I like to be alone and I don't like anyone analysing my reactions to things. I bought a digital test – it was 2007. I can't believe they already had them, they seem so cutting edge to me, even today.

I went to the toilet, pissed on the stick, pissed on my fingers, wondered what I was gonna wear that weekend, thought about how funny Jules looked the night before curled up on the couch, stoned out of his brain, looked down and saw the word **Pregnant** on the piss-covered stick.

My first thought? Oh my God. I'm having a baby.

I wasn't even that stressed. Jules and I were a funny couple like that. We had nothing, wanted for nothing and just kind of went with it. I guess you could say we were both as irresponsible as each other. I got home and told him. He was stoked and told the whole house – one day it's an STD, the next it's a baby. We all cheered and drank to a new baby… well, I didn't drink. Jules called his mum, announced that we were coming to England for a holiday and bringing a bun in the oven.

She was like, "What? Who?"

He was like, "Oh, my new girlfriend, Con."

So we set off. I knew we wouldn't last. I didn't really know what I was doing. We went to the pub one night and I'd had no idea how boring life without booze was. I was a big drinker. I loved it, I drank until I passed out and woke up in strange places, texting my best friend while holding in my laughter and sneaking out. A humble life but a good one.

Now, I was a fun sponge, checking the time, sipping on my orange juice. Every time someone went to the bar, they would buy me another fucking juice. How much juice did they think sober people need? It reminds me of the old saying: eight glasses of water a day seems impossible, while twelve beers, a wine and a Jägermeister shot seems perfectly reasonable.

I wasn't happy. We bought our tickets, all my hard-earned money that was supposed to take me around the world to learn languages and shag Spaniards going on a holiday to suburban England with my new baby daddy. I barely knew what he looked like, I hadn't been sober since we met.

I was freaking myself out. We had already told the whole world we were having a baby. Thankfully, social media hadn't quite taken off yet and the whole world really just meant the whole pub, and let's be honest, none of them really gave a fuck.

But I had told my sister, my mum and my close friends, and they were all excited for me. None of them really expected much more from me. Before I knew it, it was time to leave. We spent a week together in Bali, where I can safely say that we fell out of love. I started feeling sick, the food there only made me feel worse and sober me didn't really love Jules at all.

One day, we were in the lobby of the hotel and he said, "Pass me your phone, I need to call my dad and my phone's fucked."

I passed him my phone and he was looking for a text message in it that his dad had sent to him. I didn't know what he was doing and said, "Are you going through my phone?"

He responded by throwing it at me, and screaming, "No, I'm looking for my dad's number but if I wanted to go through your phone, I would, coz you're my fucking girlfriend!"

No, I was no longer into this. I decided to bite my tongue until I got to England. I had no idea what I was going to do. I didn't even know the abortion laws in England. I started walking, I must have walked halfway around the island, patting stray dogs and meeting locals, getting followed home by creeps, while Jules drank at the bar.

We were strangers living completely different experiences, and we quickly decided that when we got to England, I'd spend a bit of time getting to know his parents and then we'd go our separate ways. And I had no idea what way that would be.

By the time we landed in Manchester, I was so sick from a combination of morning sickness and food poisoning that I collapsed in the customs line and had to be carried by security to the front of the line. I always think about that when I'm in customs now – fake collapsing.

We got our luggage and waiting for us at the gate was Jules's dad, Marty. Now, I wasn't expecting to fall in love with Jules's family. Families generally hated me, and I hated them. I was always the bad influence, so in the end I just played up to it and purposely freaked families out before they had the chance to reject me. But Marty... the way he hugged his boy Jules with tears in his eyes, and warmly greeted me, carrying my bags, opening the door for me... something about the whole family relaxed me so much that as soon as I got in the car, I fell straight to sleep. I heard him talking about how exhausted I looked and I never wanted to leave. I stayed asleep for the entire hour-long journey it took to get to his house, just outside of Manchester from the airport.

His mum was no different, so welcoming. She only had one daughter and three sons and was the most "mumsy" mum I had ever met. I don't know if they were just a comfortable alternative to a scary reality or if I was just feeling vulnerable, but they changed my mind about Jules and gave me second thoughts. Maybe we could have this baby.

When Jules was honest with his family that we were thinking about separating and not having the baby, they understood and were never pushy.

I remember waking up one morning and Jules's mum was on the end of my bed with a cup of tea for me. I mean, really, this was one of the best things that had ever happened to me. I was being doted on by this angel. She made me pea and ham soup, comforted me and took me shopping. I almost forgot that Jules existed and jumped into her bed at night.

Then Jules made the mistake of hiring a car for a road trip into London, sightseeing, like double-decker buses and the Tower of London.

As Queen Oprah puts it, "There are no mistakes, because you are part of a supreme destiny. There are no wrong paths, there is no such thing as failure, it's just there to point you in a different direction. Feelings of uneasiness are just there to let you know it's time to change direction."

THE RECKLESS BEHAVIOUR
OF A LOST QUEEN

As I sat on that double-decker bus, surrounded by American and Australian tourists, I could only think of one thing: Javier. He lived on these streets, he would be playing music in some underground bar somewhere, filming something that only he recognised the beauty in, talking shit about how much he hates this town but could never leave, charming someone who wasn't me. I scanned the streets with my eyes. Jules had no idea what I was doing. I obviously wasn't going to bump into him, this wasn't St Kilda, you didn't just bump into people you knew. After a two-hour tour of not seeing anything but a hell of a lot of long-haired people, defeated, I turned back to Jules. It was time to go back to the hotel, so that we could wake up early and head home… just after I watched him sink a few pints at the pub.

Fuck. This.

A few days later, I couldn't sleep. I had waited to be here for so long, I longed for London. I could still smell it. Everything happens in London.

When I first met Javier, I told him I didn't want to go to London, that I wasn't interested, I wanted to go straight to Italy, then Spain, Romania and Croatia… but not London. He told me I was dreaming, he told me to think of Europe as a cafe and in that cafe, London is the pinboard. It's the place you have to go to see what's going on in the rest of the world. You're allowed to hate it, but you can't avoid it.

And there it was, the pinboard presenting itself to me with all of its opportunities and, most of all, Javier. Just to smell him again, to let him tell me a story, to make him laugh one more time would be everything to me. Maybe it was Jules's behaviour, or maybe the fact that I just didn't love him, or maybe it was the fact that I wasn't over Javier. I was too young to know what I did and didn't consider normal or respectful. I didn't enjoy being around Jules; he disregarded my situation, but didn't all men do that? Wasn't it normal to fall pregnant and move to a different planet from your partner? Looking back of course it wasn't. But so many times in my life I've passed off unhappiness as normal.

I told Jules that I had to go, that he had to let me go, that I would be back but I needed to experience London. He agreed. He knew that we were over. I wasn't sure if he was upset or not; some days, he would cry and ask me if we could try harder and other days he would play his old drum set all day, ignore me and flirt with other women when we went out. One night, at the pub together, he even asked me if he could take home a chick he'd met. She winked at me and I just walked back to his house, cold and sober. The next day, I got dressed, went to the train station and caught a train into London by myself.

I asked a stranger what stop was the best one for central London and he told me King's Cross. I got off there, turned left and kept walking until I found a hotel. I walked inside and booked myself a room. It was gross, smelt like smoke and I imagined a lot of gross men had taken poor prostitutes in between the sheets, but I didn't care. I was free… well, as free as I could be.

I got dressed into something that made me feel human again and I walked to the nearest payphone – my phone still had my prepaid Aussie SIM in it and didn't work. But there was one thing I did have. The sentimental lover inside me had never deleted text messages that I had received months earlier from Javier, messages that said: **I love you my baby, beso.**

After a while of figuring out this money system, I put a pound in the payphone and dialled the number, thinking, "Surely he has another number, or is in Spain or America… fuck, maybe he's even in Asia… "

"Hello?"

…

…

…

"It's Constance. What are you doing tonight?"

"What? Are you kidding me? Is this a joke? In London? You weren't getting here for months. Fuuuuuuuuuck baby! I'm at work. Give me half an hour and meet me at a bar in Soho. Can you get there?"

Of course I could get there. I got here, I could get anywhere he told me to. I caught my first and last cab in London and waited outside the bar he told me to meet him at. Soho blew me away. It was cold but people were everywhere: colourful people, people from everywhere. Some were sober, some were off their heads, gays were comfortable to hold hands, fetish shops were open and luring people in.

I was in my element – adventure, love, uncertainty – my heaven. As I saw him walking up the street, I ran towards him. He picked me up and we both grinned at each other before he planted a huge kiss on my lips. Of course he took me to the coolest place in town. Despite not being a big drinker and certainly not a party animal, he knew where to go. I had a drink, but only one.

Javier had two before he told me to fess up. "Come on, you can tell me."

I thought he had noticed that I was pregnant. I was only eight weeks at this point but it wasn't like me to be in a bar for more than thirty minutes and not be sculling, dancing, or looking for something to spike my drink with.

But it was something else that he noticed.

"You have a man, don't you baby?" he said with such nonchalant composure that it kind of burnt. It wasn't until later in my life, where I'd be with a man with actual jealousy issues, that I learnt it is not in fact a sign of love. While a small amount of jealousy is healthy, any more than that is nothing but a debilitating headache.

I didn't lie. I told him; after all, he was the one who requested a non-committal, long-distance, might-never-see-each-other-again thing.

We spoke about everything; well, kind of everything. I told him that I had gotten myself in a relationship and was now changing my mind about it, and he understood. If anyone understands falling in and out of love, it's Javier. He had no major confessions to make. He played his cards and love life close to his chest, never letting anyone completely in, and never keeping anyone completely out. I told him everything except the small fact that I was pregnant.

Then he asked me if I was taking him home. I couldn't say no, or wouldn't say no. Either way, I didn't say no.

I know. You are all hating me right now.

We caught the train back to my hotel and Javier told me that he felt I had grown up, matured. He said that he remembered me being a big party girl and was so impressed that I had sat on one drink all night. He actually had no idea how much I wanted to be drunk. The only thing that killed the boredom was the butterflies I had in my stomach over the fact that I was actually with the love of my life again, in his presence, hand in hand. I was living in the now, not worried about a thing.

When we arrived at my hotel, I told him which number my room was and he went to buy a bottle of red while I took myself up to my room.

I answered the door in a tiny black lace nightie; the idea of doing that now just makes me piss myself laughing. We sat on the bed, he grabbed my hair and pulled it back and I just died. I had missed him so much and I loved him so much… and here I was next to him, finally.

We made out, we kissed and he whispered in my ear that I was finally back with him, that we were finally together again, he even whispered that he couldn't believe I had a boyfriend and had forgotten about him.

Fuck, as if I had forgotten him.

And that's when I had to stop.

The anxiety was killing me. I was unable to go any further. All I kept thinking about was the fact that there was a baby in my tummy. I didn't understand the ethics around the whole situation, a baby had been put there by one dick, and another dick was about to be hanging around up there – did people do that?

Javier never needed to get pushy. He didn't have a problem picking up chicks and at the end of the day, we were friends and lovers, and we did more than just fuck. I stayed with him, falling in love with the same man for the second time in my life. I would have done anything he told me to do.

Before I went to sleep, I said to him, "I can't believe you told me to give you thirty minutes when I called today, you should have just jumped up and said, 'where are you?'"

He responded, "I was at work. I needed that thirty minutes to go and buy new socks and jocks so I could come home with you."

Yep, I'd do anything this man told me to do… and he knew it.

I woke up in the morning filled with anxiety. I made Javier leave ten minutes before me and I explained to him what Jules looked like and told him to keep walking if he was there. Jules didn't even know where I was staying, but the guilt made me believe he had superpowers.

Javier couldn't understand why I wasn't just running away with him. He had already offered to get me a room in the hostel that he lived in; it was cheap there and I could stay in the room that he shared with his best friend whenever I wanted to.

I told him I'd think about it, that I had things to take care of first. He didn't pry, he kissed me goodbye and made me promise I'd call him.

I caught the train back to Jules's house and sat in a silent confusion for the whole day. Jules asked me if I'd come out to dinner with his mates that night. I agreed and we went out for curry. The English are crazy about their curry, I had no idea, I didn't even know what to order. Today, it's my favourite food.

One of Jules's friends asked me what kind of food I liked, and I told him "sweet stuff" so he ordered me a korma. All of Jules's friends knew about the baby and were really happy for us.

We silently went along with it, knowing that the baby probably wasn't going to be born. An abortion was its most likely destiny. Had I bonded with the baby? No. Was I excited about the baby? Not anymore. Now that Jules and I pretty much couldn't stand each other, I knew it wasn't right. I ate my korma and needed to shit, so I excused myself.

I got into the toilets, sat down, pulled down my pants and… didn't need to shit. I stood up and felt an incredible pain tearing through my abdomen. I had no idea what it was, it kind of felt like period pain but I had no idea why. I squatted in the toilets and broke out into a sweat. I actually thought that the korma hadn't agreed with me. I tried to shit again. Nothing but a bit of wee. I went to wipe my fanny and saw a strange, deep-coloured blood on the toilet paper. Now, back then I didn't have any mates who had been pregnant, nor did I have Google, but I had watched enough movies to know this wasn't a good sign.

And the pain grew and grew. I had mixed emotions between not wanting anyone to come into the toilet out of concern for me, to being incredibly worried myself. After about twenty minutes I stood up, sucked it up and went out to sit with Jules. I nudged him and told him I was bleeding.

He was just as clueless as me and we just sat there in more silence. When we got home, we went straight to bed and pretended the whole evening hadn't happened.

The next day, Jules parents had invited his family over to meet me, how lovely. I was in a world of confusion and misery. I just wanted to be free to live the most selfish version of the 22-year-old me and I was confronted with so many conflicting avenues to choose from. I went to have my morning piss and there was even more blood, some bright red, and some brown.

I called out to Jules. He knew what I was going to say and really didn't want to deal with it, so he sent his beautiful mum into the bathroom. She ran me a shower and told me that the baby might not be gone, that plenty of women bleed. I told her that I had wanted an abortion but now that the baby had chosen to leave because I'm such a fuck-up, I kind of wished it wouldn't. She stroked my hair and told me that what will be will be, the less I stress, the better. Such kindness, I really couldn't understand it, I couldn't understand her. Why was she being so nice to me when her son and I hated each other? Was I pregnant, or wasn't I? Why was I spending all of this time investing in Jules's family? We both know we were over; we were fun and we worked but then we weren't fun and we didn't work.

That's how you know that a relationship works, when the fun stops but the love doesn't. Fortunately for most of us, the fun doesn't really stop until we get pregnant, but if the love stops then, we are up shit creek – either trying to pretend it hasn't stopped, or working really hard to keep the relationship alive.

Jules and I left it for a couple of days. Not knowing what was going on, we went to the local doctor. I told him that I thought I'd had a miscarriage, and he told me that there was nothing he could do to save the baby if I'd had one. I told him that was fine, we had decided that we didn't want the baby anymore but we just need to know what the baby was doing.

To which he replied that he couldn't refer me to an abortion clinic, it was against his religion. And that was that.

Take two. We went to another doctor. I was still bleeding and cramping; she was kind and gave me a referral to an abortion clinic. We told them our dilemma and they saw me the following day.

Having an abortion in a foreign country, to a guy that you feel like you hardly know, is bizarre. The whole thing felt bizarre. I don't remember much. I remember it was free, I remember they put a suppository up my arse for the pain, I remember that the minute I woke up I ran to the toilet and shat it out and I remember that Jules and I looked at each other afterwards with a fundamental knowledge that we had done the right thing and we were over. No hard feelings.

The next day, I packed my things. His parents gave me hugs, his mum handed me a present that she had gotten for me to give my mum, and his dad handed me his phone number, warning me that England is a big place and if I ever needed anything to come back, I was welcome, and they were there.

I called Javier, told him I was coming back, and he booked me a bed in the hostel somewhere in London, a pretty shitty area but it was classic London and had beds for eight pounds a night, at a time London was booming.

Jules and I had return tickets booked for four weeks after I left him. Obviously I had no intention of catching that plane. I had six months stamped on my passport and I intended on using them. Only I had no work permit, fuck all money now and no return flights.

On the day that our plane was leaving, I received a text message to the English phone number that I had bought. It was Jules: **I'm catching our flight, are you ok?**

To which I replied: **Yeah I'm fine, not coming home though. Are you ok?**

He responded: **I'm fine now that I know you're ok.**

And that was it. I won't say I've never wondered what would have happened if we made different choices and I have certainly always wondered if that baby was still alive in my tummy when we had the abortion. People often ask me if I've had a miscarriage and I frankly don't know. Did I send it away or did it decide to leave me and my fucked-up circumstances?

AT THE END OF THE DAY, ALL YOU HAVE IS YOU

Living out of a backpack is where I'm happiest: not knowing where I'm sleeping, living, or where my next meal comes from. It silences all of the noise in my head.

I spent my days with headphones on. I bought myself a pair of going-out shoes from Primark (a big cheap retail outlet) for two pounds, and a headscarf off an African fella selling them at the train station. Three different modelling agent scouts stopped me and said they could find me work and, while healthy for the ego, it didn't match my "deep" traveller theme.

I wrote every day. I wrote Javier love letters, I wrote and rewrote comments that passers-by said to me, I wrote out my favourite lyrics to an Arctic Monkeys song fifty times until it sunk in properly, I went to bars with enough money for one beer and my Moleskine diary, and I fell in love with London and with Javier.

He would take me to museums on his days off, hire a car and drive me up the coast on his weekends off. He taught me things and showed me things. But then I went back to my old ways and left his workmates unimpressed as I pissed myself laughing on the dancefloor after slipping over on a jug at his after-work drinks.

I was lucky enough to find a bar in central London with a sleazy owner who couldn't believe his luck when I walked through the door; an English-speaking Aussie, willing to work for nothing.

I started to party more and grew bored of the sobriety that Euro life brought me. I missed my home, where we stand around a backyard bonfire figuring out which lucky man we were gonna try and root – if we don't spew first. Some nights, we got both; those blokes were the real troupers.

But alas, Javier was judging me… and looking back, I'd judge me too. But I couldn't see it at the time. I just wanted to be loved for me.

One night, when I got home from work, Javier and his bestie were asleep in bed, and still buzzed from the bar I worked at, I thought it was wise to go to the pub downstairs and drink with an Aussie chick I met. Fuck, I must have drunk a whole bottle of wine in like thirty minutes and then moved on to shooters. In my mind, everyone in the bar thought I was a legend. So when I stumbled back into our room I turned the light on and proceeded to be hilarious and glamorous (fucked-up and not funny) to Javier and his mate, they rolled their eyes and went back to sleep. I snuggled up to Javier, love me, love me, love me. He did not love me.

I felt pretty shit when he told me in the morning that I had made the whole room smell like booze and cigarettes. I was like a drunk hobo ruining the sleep of these two Roman gods.

And so began the decline.

I couldn't stop fucking up in Javier's eyes. The more I'd fuck up, the more he wouldn't love me, and the less he loved me, the more I'd fuck up. He moved to Cambridge – I think to get away from me. The guy who owned the pub I worked at gave me a room in another pub on Kilburn High Road.

Javier promised he'd visit when he came back to London, which was supposed to be quite regularly. Only one last fuck-up would ensure that would never happen.

I knew he had met someone else; he always met someone else. He was seeing someone in the hostel we stayed in when I first arrived in London, but tried to hide it from me. One night she and I were drinking, and she told me. She was lovely and heartbroken. I had also found out that when I met him in Melbourne, he'd had a girlfriend who had just left.

Yet I couldn't leave him, he was magnetic. But like all magnets, he had his repelling side, and that was commitment. He didn't want to commit, and he also didn't want the wild child I was exposing myself as.

This particular night, he promised to call me. He didn't, and I'm not the type to hang around. When things go bad, I go. I don't beg or let myself look like a loser... usually...

I decided I was bored in my room so I went to the only area that I really knew, Soho. I took myself on a date... alright, a pub crawl. I bought myself pints and red wines and talked to everyone that would listen. It started out fun and I was planning to go home after my third pub. I would spend the next year of my life wishing I had gone home.

Walking through the streets, an Italian restaurant owner was closing his restaurant and drinking on the street. He was loud, calling out to everyone who would listen, trying to lure them in for free wine. I was the prime candidate, one bottle, two bottles... I started sending Javier messages that didn't make sense. They were like The Da Vinci Code; nobody could crack them. My memory of the night was as sketchy as an etch-a-sketch but I do remember a few things.

I left the restaurant absolutely maggoted, and I walked and walked through the streets of London. It was a Saturday night and I'd never seen anything like it.

I knew it was time to go home but I had no idea how I would get there. I went to a cab rank that had no cabs and shitloads of pissed punters at it. I asked police to help me, but they ignored me. I asked a black chick and she was about to help me when her mate screamed at her that a pretty little white Aussie cunt would never help them in Australia, not exactly a good point considering I'd definitely help her.

Finally, an Indian-looking bloke offered to help me and asked me if I was lost. Pissed and confused, with tears on my cheeks, I told him I was, I told him I knew the name of my street but that was it.

He said, "Follow me."

And I did. I followed him down the road, around the corner, down an alleyway, behind a casino and near a skip bin in the back streets, where a white van was waiting for me. He kicked it and opened the back and inside was another man. They looked like they could be brothers.

He reached out for my hand and said, "Come in."

I hesitated. The other guy said, "Come on we are taking you home".

My life flashed before my eyes. I turned and I ran and ran and ran, until I felt the safety of streetlights and nightclubs and cars again.

I was cold. I wanted Australia. I was regretting everything, all the dumb life choices I had made. I just wanted a familiar face. I sat on the curb, put my bag by my feet and I cried. What more could go wrong? I was a wreck. No wonder Javier wasn't by my side. Who would want to be with a mess like me? I had no substance, no direction. My only real want was to fuck myself over, because I clearly didn't value myself. I clearly only valued myself on whatever man's arm I was hanging off and without one, I was just a crying drunken mess on the curb in London.

And just when things couldn't get any worse, someone grabbed my bag. I didn't have money. I don't come from money, I had no jewels, my phone was ten pounds from the post office, but do you know what I had? I had rollies, my journal and my passport. Three things that no fucker was taking from me.

Surprising myself, I looked up, jumped and grabbed that op-shop leather satchel and yanked it back to its rightful owner... only to be booted in the face by a dodgy sneaker, worn by the fuckrag who had tried to take it.

And the fight in me just kept coming. Fuck this town and fuck men and fuck this cunt!

I jumped up, pushed him and screamed in his face. I don't know what I yelled, probably something classy along the lines of how I was gonna smash this motherfucker in the head if he didn't back off, I'm not one to be fucked with and I've been fucked with A LOT tonight...

And he turned and he ran. And I regained a tiny piece of power and control for myself.

I turned around and walked to the casino I had passed while trying not to get human trafficked and I spoke to the security guard. I told him my situation and showed him my swollen eye. He called one of the staff members and asked him to take me home.

The staff member took me home. He was kind and gave me a pep talk about getting my shit together, about seeming like a smart girl… a beautiful girl…and as I got out, he asked me if he could take me out that week.

"Ha ha ha ha ha," I laughed and closed the door.

Fuck men.

I woke up in the morning and felt even more sorry for myself as I did the dreaded text message catch-up to find out exactly how tragic I had been.

Yep, I had texted Javier, had told him I was lost, abandoned, hurt, nearly dead. Oh, the drama.

He had tried to call me fifteen times, but this precious snowflake was getting her beauty sleep. Deep, deep, deep passed-out sleep.

I returned his call and he was furious.

"I don't want to be with you anymore. You are a mess. Being with Constance is to never know where she is or whom she is with. I thought you were dead. And I'm done."

"Please," I pleaded. "Let me come to Cambridge today, let me show you that I'm not a mess, I love you so much."

"No, don't come. I don't want to see you again."

And so I did what all tragic stalkers would do. I went to Cambridge, I tried to cover my bruise with makeup, I even ate, even though food was something I considered a waste of money at this point in my life. I ate a big salad roll to try to cover up the smell of stale alcohol on my breath and I caught a train to Cambridge. I had no idea where he lived there so I called him from a payphone as I had run out of credit.

He answered coz it was a private number and he couldn't tell it was me, and I begged him, I told that I had nobody, nothing, that he owed me to at least say goodbye to my face.

And finally he agreed, coming to the train station on a bike. I realised then he had no intention of letting come to his house, of letting me in. He rode next to me as he showed me Cambridge and started to refer to us in past tense.

I looked at him, his long hair, his beautiful Spanish face, his big white teeth and I said to him, "That's it then? There is nothing I can do to keep you?"

And he responded, "There are two things I hate: girls who smell like alcohol and girls who don't take care of themselves. Right now, you are both."

Fuck him and fuck that salad roll.

My heart broke and I cried for weeks. I sent him dumb messages. He had showed me what a loser I really could be. I cried the first time I slept with another man, many months later. And finally, just when I thought I never would, I started to heal.

I moved to Spain.

I got lost in Spain.

I moved back to Australia.

Settled down.

I fell in and out of love a few more times.

I got married.

I had two babies; babies that changed everything.

I found myself: in my work, my love, my children's eyes.

I took fewer risks, put up stronger boundaries.

I loved me. I became someone I was proud to be, I became the mother I always wanted to be, I was relaxed and free and happiest when my babies were in my arms.

Seven years passed. Until the day my phone beeped. I was sitting at dinner with my old friend and her new boyfriend. A random number and a text message that said: **Your new salon looks cool, I drove past it. Javier.**

My heart stopped. Why? Why would he even be here, how

could he be here? This is the arse-end of the world for him. Last I'd heard, he was living in Spain.

My friend asked me what was wrong, that I looked like I had seen a ghost. I handed her my phone.

"What are you gonna do?"

"Nothing, of course. I don't need this headfuck. I'm finally not a crazy woman anymore."

"Don't you kind of want to show him that you're not crazy anymore?"

"Nah. Chances are, I'll go crazy again."

We both knew that was for the best.

In fact, I stuck to it for a good couple of months but I just couldn't help myself. I didn't want to spend the rest of my life wondering.

Would I lose my mind? Start acting crazy? Would he send me crazy?

As a mum, these kinds of encounters are off-limits. Who could parent and fall in love? There just aren't that many hours in the day. My brain is full, not to mention my heart.

But what's in a coffee?

So I went.

Javier, looking every bit the man who broke me – never ageing, just getting better – looked at me with his cheeky, I-get-away-with-everything face and melted me with, "I was put on this earth to kiss your pussy."

I knew he was right. He was put on this earth to kiss my pussy… and many other pussies, and I was absolutely OK with that. I didn't see him as a god anymore. There were no hard feelings and there was still so much love, but he's not one to be tied down or be committed to, at least not by me.

And me? Ironically, I had become the woman Javier had always wanted me to be. I never binge drink, I'm committed to my life, because I loved it and I loved me.

And I realised that I had only now just learnt what real love was. I would have done anything for Javier – if he told me kill, I would have killed. Only he told me to love, and I just couldn't; I couldn't love me, for him.

Then along came my kids. In order to love them and give them what they deserved, I needed to love me. So I did. I learnt to love me and became someone I could easily love, in order to love them.

All the heartache, all the ups and downs, chasing men around the world, writing about love in my journals, pouring my heart out to a glass of pinot. It wasn't for nothing. I had to go around and around and around in so many circles and hit my head against so many brick walls before I could pick my shit up, look in the mirror and learn: it was me all along. I was the one I had to fall in love with and with that, I found love.

If only it hadn't taken heartache, chlamydia, abortion/ miscarriage, more heartache, black eyes and a world of travelling to finally realise that I was the answer all along.

Love is not what the movies and the songs lead us to believe. Love doesn't hurt, it doesn't leave you crying in hostels or sending passionate love letters to boys that don't write back.

Love is strength, consistency and consideration. Love is sacrificing the good pillow. Love is knowing that love will be there in the morning. Love is seeing a haemorrhoid on your lover's arse, and instead of getting grossed out, naming it Bruce.

AND THEN ALONG CAME DENIM

ALONG CAME DENIM

The say all's fair in love and war, but time and time again all women know of love is war, and how is that ever fair?

I knew it was love the minute I rested my head in his nook. You know the nook? It's that place in between a man's shoulder and his chest, which appears to have been designed perfectly for your head. A heartbeat resounded through my head. Have you ever heard a heartbeat that sent a chill down your spine? As a kid I used to rest my head on my mum's boobs and listen to her breathing, in and out. Only my mum's love meant so much to me that every breath sent a chilling fear that it was my responsibility to listen out for a wheeze or a cough, one that could be the beginning of her end. So I'd sit there listening to her breath while holding my own.

I never thought I'd be here, 33 years old, a mother of four, listening to a heartbeat, a heartbeat that I only knew had existed for a couple of short months, and praying with everything I had that it never stop. While I rest my head in the only place I ever want to rest my head again, his nook. Talking myself into letting love be the only thing I have never let it be – Love.

We both know that our love won't come without a war and I don't know how fair that is. What I do know is that with this love we'll be fighting on the same side of the war. It will be us against them. Us against the world and we might just win.

*

I was out for dinner. Well, not dinner. I was feeding the kids. As part of my slow transformation into my mother, I rarely eat dinner.

It was at the local pub, only a short walk from my house, which is part of the reason I bought the place. I arrange dinners with friends there all the time, partly so I can have a wine and bitch about my life, and partly because a kid's pasta is $8 and you can't even buy the ingredients for bolognese for that price.

The added bonus is that you are not home for "cunt hour" – the hour between 5 and 6pm that leaves a mother suicidal or rocking in the corner of her house, hiding from the deformed, mutant children she somehow spawned.

The kids were skating in the car park. They hadn't touched their pasta, a lot less painful when you're merely paying for it and not slaving over the hot fucking stove.

A friend and I decided to grab some takeaways and head up to the skate park to exhaust the kids and minimise our chances of bringing "cunt hour" home with us.

We pulled up and got out of the car. It wasn't a cold night. I was wearing high-waisted shorts, a tank top and thongs. Don't ask me why I remember these sorts of details, but I could pretty much tell you what I was wearing to every single event in my life. I walked over to where the parents sit, where two dads were watching their kids skate. The sun was going down, and it's not common for parents to be there after dark; usually it's just me, my kids and some teenagers huddled in the corner trying their luck at a can bong.

My friend knew the dads – Margaret River is a small town –

but before she even had the chance to introduce us one of them said, "Now here is a familiar face. Constance Hall."

I am used to being recognised. In our family, we call it being "Queened". It's the reason that I am never the one to go into the post office but wait in the car; the reason I am exempt from petrol paying duties. Not because I don't love it, but quite the opposite, I love it too much, and it takes over our day and I never get anything done. It's been a couple of years now. I love these women, and they love me. It's a major part of my life.

What I'm not used to, what completely took me by surprise that night was that this time, it was by a man – Denim, a local single dad. I hadn't met him or heard of him before this night. But he knew who I was.

He was sitting on a really uncomfortable bench at the skate park, wearing jeans and a dark blue hoody with his hair pulled back, and sat for most of the time that we chatted with his hands in the pockets of his jumper.

He introduced me to his mate and to his kids. I tried to introduce him to my kids, but all they ever do in the company of adults is embarrass the shit out of me by refusing to speak, or by screaming at me, so I leave them as a hidden surprise at the end of any new meeting.

Denim's children were a different story, kind and caring. They were little pro-skaters; everyone else pretty much stood back holding their boards, watching them in awe. Denim's mate was trying to get his little boy into the car, and his eldest son Sunny swooped him up, holding him, tickling him and put him in the car. They were so sweet, so helpful.

Arlo yelled at me, told me I was the worst mum in the world because he had fallen off his fucking skateboard – go figure.

We talked for a while. At one point, Denim's kid came to sit with us and Denim introduced me saying, "This is Constance. Do you remember me telling you about that blogger from Perth who has heaps of followers yet never sells out? She doesn't have any sponsors or paid posts on her Facebook page?" His son nodded politely.

It was so intriguing to meet a man who not only knew who I was, but appreciated what I did. I have been offered easy money for paid posts, but it's just never felt right. I look at celebrities; they have acting careers, comedy careers, singing or whatever. I have nothing but my followers, so that kind of makes them my only asset. All I have is my honesty with them, which makes them the only thing I won't sell.

Not to mention I have the smartest followers in the world. If I turned around tomorrow and said, "Oh my God, this baking tray is seriously the best thing I have ever bought! I'm wet just thinking about how easily I bake with it, not to mention how easy it is to clean, just thinking about washing this motherfucker brings me to climax."

NO. Just no.

Trust me, sometimes I've needed the money. People never see that. They'd crucify you if you did it but they never notice when you don't. Denim noticed.

I have this thing, this skill, this knack. I've never really noticed it about myself before, but Denim is constantly pointing it out. I draw info out of people; they open up to me. It might be the hairdresser in me. I used to call it the magic cape – you put it on and everyone spills their guts. Honestly, there is nothing callous about it, I am just so interested in other people's lives, in particular their love lives. It takes me on average about 45 seconds to find out someone's relationship status, not just if they're in a relationship but if they are actually happy, how long they have been together, personal details of their past relationships. Don't worry, it's not a one-way street; I divulge too.

I asked Denim where the boys' mum was; not because I was interested in him, but I was really just interested in knowing where she was. You would think I'd have been imagining a long-haired hippy woman who was about to pull up in a Kombi and claim her man, but I wasn't. Something about the way Denim spoke about himself and the boys, part of me knew she wasn't exactly in the picture.

And then he told me, "She passed away."

As horrified as anyone is when they find out that a woman passed away leaving behind her babies, I asked how she died, to which he responded, "Suicide."

Everything changed, and it wasn't sympathy. It was almost a feeling that all mothers can relate to; when you find out that a child doesn't have a mum, you kind of connect with that mum and feel the need to look out for them. Despite this dad doing what looked like an incredible job, I felt the mothering urge surge through me.

I daresay a lot of women have had the same feeling when they meet these boys with their caring, loveable natures. You can't imagine that it all comes from their dad. Only when you get to know them do you realise that they get everything they need from their dad.

Denim was different with my kids. He pointed out straight away that Arlo was pushing with the wrong foot on his board; he asked my daughter what happened when she came climbing up the ramp sobbing over a fall. Denim is such a big kid himself that he just jumps straight in with kids. I've since learnt that he's actually a lot more comfortable around them, and rather than fumbling through an adult conversation about something that would probably bore the shit out of him, he just heads straight to the kids and teaches them a skate trick or gives them a boost up a tree.

So many men these days back away from other people's kids. It must be hard for them, always thinking they are being second-guessed and scared of being accused of being a pedo when they so much as help a kid tie her shoelaces.

Denim was different; he was sure of himself, sure of himself around me, and sure of himself around kids. The more he spoke to me, the more I learnt how amazing he was.

He told me only a few details about their journey to heal, a trip they took around Australia against all advice, with child protection chasing him to put the kids back in school, with no money and no direction, on a quest to do whatever makes the kids happy, and that happened to be skating every single skate park around Australia.

They would drive and skate. If they ran out of money, they would park by a skate park until they got paid again. Sunny told me that they would skate until they couldn't walk.

The story blew me away. I felt connected to Denim but I had no idea on what level. The kids were so captivating, I asked him if he would mind if I wrote about his story; he told me not at all. I asked him to friend request me, he handed me his phone and told me he had no idea how to do that, so I friend requested myself on his phone.

My kids then embarrassed me for the final time that evening, so I excused myself, threw my empty cider into the bin, rounded up the kids and jumped into the car – not knowing that soon my whole world was going to change.

I jumped into bed, accepted Denim's friend request and read the status on his page that said:

After a random crossing of paths tonight I can happily report and confirm that Constance Hall is every bit the Queen that she professes. Without tarnishing my masculine ruggedness I confess to enjoying her honesty, and often funny posts, and happily admit that she inspires me too.

Real life Con was the same, smart, funny, honest, down to earth humble human that I knew she would be… She exudes a wonderful beauty and sharing a few short life stories was an effortless pleasure.

Made my night, hope our paths cross again.

Little did we know that our two paths would more than cross.

How are you supposed to recognise your destiny when your mind is closed? If you wait in the car, get on your phone to avoid people, say hi and keep walking? I didn't have to sit with Denim; I could have waited in my car. So often I would have buried myself in solitude. But how are you supposed to hear two souls saying, "I thought you'd never come," if you don't give them a chance to recognise each other?

Stay open every day: to the shop assistant and the other mums at school, even to the dickhead who pulled out in front of you. Connections tap you on the shoulder all the time.

ALWAYS ALONE BUT NEVER LONELY

The majority of women leaving a relationship don't need to learn to be alone – they learn that in their relationship. Nothing teaches you how to start enjoying your own company like being in a miserable marriage. People don't come over, you don't go out. You spend your nights alone and your days alone, so you become quite good at being alone.

I was alone until two young family members moved in to help me with the twins while I worked. They shared a bedroom in my three-bedroom house and everyone else just fit in. A camper trailer was pitched around the side of my house for my nomadic stepdad to stay in whenever he was in town. Even I would think we were trailer trash if I walked past.

My new nannies and I saved each other. They were coming out of shitty relationships, I was newly single, and we all kind of came together to make it work. I gave them somewhere to live and a job, they gave me the freedom to work and have some kind of a life of my own.

I used to have the worst alone issues. I would go from relationship to relationship, frantically searching for someone who could make me feel like me, and reflect me, which sounds so dumb now. I know it was the stupidest thing to do, but my need to be with someone at all times stopped me from making rational decisions, decisions that I wouldn't regret and that wouldn't hurt people I loved. Selfish decisions, but I was in a very selfish time of my life.

I wonder if that happens to many women who have been selflessly mothering for a few years and then *BAM*, they make up for it in a few short months. Take back all of that Mother Teresa crap, dancing on tables, popping champagne and winking at men who are pretending they don't see.

I went to therapy to try to resolve my alone issues, only to find out that there is actually nothing wrong with enjoying company and wanting to share your life – some people find strength in solitude, others draw strength from keeping people close. It's who you have near you that makes it a healthy or unhealthy situation. If you are always attracted to people who need you to help them, people who are draining your finances or energy, people who are an all-round negative influence on your behaviour, you might want to have a look at it. If you're simply keeping people close for strength and humour, and a general bounce around of ideas, then great, keep them close. There are no rules.

I was lucky enough to cross paths with a survivor of domestic violence, Mary. She had been bruised and battered, treated like a possession and in fear for her life for ten years. Ten years with a violent man can destroy the strongest of women. Mary explained to me that she didn't know how to leave, she was convinced she was trapped.

And she was. Until you have lived through domestic violence, you will never understand the invisible cage you're locked in. Other people can't get their heads around it. "Why didn't you just leave?" is a statement Mary frequently hears but statistically, victims of domestic violence are three times more likely to be killed in the months following their separation. If one thing is more scary than staying, it's leaving.

So Mary waited and prayed for a miracle, and it came. Only it was in the form of new love. She met Mark, a man she worked with. He believed in her and they fell in love and it gave her the strength to feel safe enough to leave. To this day, Mary and Mark are happily married and she believes that had she not met Mark, she would be dead.

And she laughs to me that even after all the abuse, all of the threats, her friends still thought she should have waited before getting into another relationship, to do the "right" thing. Mary taught me that everyone is different. Time alone to reflect can give some women strength, but equally, having people around to love and bounce off can give other women strength. Who are we to judge?

Me? I need people. The thought of leaving any relationship to live in an empty house with just my kids and a bottle of wine is so depressing. I didn't invite my nannies to live with me with the intention of gaining personal strength, but with them there, for the first time in years I found myself full – full of laughter, conversations and late-night cups of tea. We watched TV shows together, and laughed at *Married at First Sight*. I could go to the shops without my kids and we all made dinner together with the music on. It was kind of like being in a relationship, only it was better. It was a commune.

Don't worry about *how* someone left an unhappy relationship, just be grateful that they did. Instead of seeing ethics and morals, see one more free woman. See kids who no longer fall asleep blocking their ears. See the pattern discontinued. See children who can grow up accustomed to respect and kindness, instead of manipulation and shame.

Nobody needs to know why you left. Nobody needs to know why you stayed. It's not your job to explain it to them. Your job is to be kind to the one person who will always be there for you. You.

A RELATIONSHIP EPIPHANY: WHAT I WAS DOING WRONG

I first met Katie Eden Todd when I interviewed her for my radio show. She has worked as a therapist for thirty years and specialises in relationships. I have sat in on her seminars and she also agreed to be my personal therapist. She just makes sense.

Being surrounded by so many failed relationships, and realising that many that aren't over are still miserable, I was determined to get a better understanding of where we are going wrong.

Katie has developed an approach called "Cell Mates and Soul Mates" to help us all grasp why we are banging our heads against brick walls when it comes to co-habiting and raising spawn with our romantic, and once cherished, partners. Cell Mates being the shitty relationships that so many of us find ourselves in, the ones that go around and around in circles, feeling as if we have locked each other in a cell of unhappiness. Sometimes I think about the old scenario where one of you wants to go out, the other says, "That's not fair, you were the last one to go out and leave me here with the kids." So, the following weekend they take the reins and say, "I'm going out." Only to be greeted with an argument, "Oh it's OK for you to go out but when I try I can't." So neither of you go anywhere to "keep the peace" but it's not actual peace, it's prison.

Katie takes a spiritual approach to therapy. Maybe I'm losing my mind, but the older I get, the more sense it makes to me. Maybe I'm just searching for some reason for it all, but I take comfort in spirituality more and more these days.

Our "Child"

Katie explained to me that when we are behaving irrationally, or having a tantrum, or acting out of fear, we are behaving as our "Child", that inner three-year-old who wants all of her irrational and selfish and terrified needs met.

When you feel like you are living in a cell, like you are locked in a small world, going around in circles, not able to reach your full potential, you are living a life that is ruled by your inner Child. That Child rears its head in some people all the time, and in some people occasionally.

I asked Katie once to help me, I told her that I was fighting with Denim, usually about stupid things, like our kids, or the fact that he lost my bank card and I couldn't believe that he tried to pretend it was me who'd lost it. On this one occasion, it snowballed. Denim yelled at me, I yelled at him, I saw red and said horrible things; he told me to fuck off and went to sleep in his bus (he has a bus that he took around the country parked in our driveway). I felt so abandoned, panic set in and I went outside to apologise but he still didn't come back in and that made me angry again. How dare he do this to me when it wasn't even my fault in the first place? I came back inside and cried myself to sleep.

It was the worst feeling, and it wasn't until halfway through the next day that he spoke to me. I knew I had pushed him, and I knew I was continuing to push him away, but when I saw him backing away, I panicked and tried to undo everything, but it was too late. He had completely shut down.

The truth was, I didn't want to hurt Denim – that's the last thing I wanted – but even more so I didn't want to be given the silent treatment. I can't stand the silent treatment; I can't be shut out or punished for my words. If you want to leave me, then leave me, but I won't live in a civil war.

So I told Katie the whole story.

She explained to me that I was acting in my Child. My Child was hurt, angry and throwing a tantrum, and I let her. Which hurt Denim enough to push him into his Child. You see, my Child has a loud tantrum, throws things and says mean shit. Denim's Child goes into his room and sulks. Imagine a child sulking in his room, and the friend or sibling who caused him to do it goes into his room to try and snap him out of it by… yelling more, hurting him more. Would he snap out of it? No. He'd retreat further. And what would the retreating behaviour do to the child who was angrily throwing things? Make her more upset.

So what's the answer, I asked Katie? What do we do if we are both being irrational in a fight but don't want to end up there again? And her response was life-changing: "Con, stop asking Denim to parent you. When you're worked up and you can't snap out of it, you are in your Child, and your Child is looking for an adult to parent you. And when Denim gives you the silent treatment for two days, he is a Child sulking, wanting a parent to notice how hurt he is and spoil him to make him feel better. You are both expecting the other to make you feel better.

But guess who is the only person who can make you feel better? You. And do you know what, Con? I have spent the majority of my career teaching adults how to parent their inner Child. That's a huge key to life, to being an adult."

Taken aback by her theory, of course I went on to ask her how the hell I do that? And she went on to explain, "When I'm in my Child and feeling overwhelmed, or scared, or like I'm about to do something stupid, I take myself into a room and I calm my inner Child down. With love, I give her a few minutes to snap out of it."

This made so much sense to me. I have been expecting people to make me feel better and parent my inner Child for so long, when I'm actually the only one who can do it. And since I heard this, I have recognised when my Child pops up and tries to take control. It has saved so many pointless arguments. I can honestly say that we haven't fought like that since. An expert once said to me it's not *that* a couple fights, it's *how* they fight.

We will still fight, but I won't let my Child push him into a corner, and he (hopefully) won't let his Child stay there for days.

Cell Mate Relationships

A Cell Mate relationship is usually one that is formed when your Child is in control of your life, or when your life is not in control and you revert to your Child and make irrational decisions. You can feel the moment when your Child takes the reins, you start saying dumb shit, you see yourself doing it but don't know how to stop it. "Well go then, nobody's making you stay!"

What kind of a statement is that? It's one that an angry child says when she's hurt or rejected or angry.

This is why you see so many couples in extremely volatile relationships with their first love, when you're young and have picked a partner that you're hoping will fix you and parent you, and they often see the same in you. You end up living in a relationship that goes around and around in circles: the fights, the tit-for-tat, the "he said, she said", the text wars.

Katie told me that a dead giveaway that a couple is in a Cell Mate relationship is the blame game. "But it's not *my* fault!" This is such a common sentence to come from a Child.

Cell Mate relationships leave you feeling lonely, even when you're not alone. A lot of people might be reading this now and nodding their heads, like they think they are in a Cell Mate relationship. There are only two ways out.

1) Leave.

So many people say that they stay for the kids, but the truth is that most people leave for the kids. It's so important for children to see a strong example of love – your relationship becomes their inner voice of love; what love looks like and what they should seek in love.

2) Become your own parent.

The inner child needs parenting; we need to stop looking for a partner to parent us. Learning to calm yourself down, to pick yourself up and to rationalise yourself is the biggest gift you will give yourself and it will take all the pressure off your relationship.

Stop expecting your lover to parent your inner child, and become your own parent.

Relationships are Contracts

One of the most profound things Katie taught me is that all relationships are a contract between two souls, and every contract is different. Everyone you meet, you have a pre-written contract with, a contract to teach each other something.

Not all relationship contracts are about love. Some are about teaching each other reliance, some are about healing each other, pushing each other until something is confronted. And if you have stayed for too long, that's OK because your contract might not be up. Some contracts last a couple of days, others last twenty years, and some are about pure love, Soul Mates that last an eternity.

What a relief. There is no such thing as a failed marriage, just a fulfilled contract. All of your contracts are intertwined with everyone that you know; it's your job to be the best version of you so that you can carry out your contracts to the best of your ability and everyone gets the best out of you, while you get the best out of them.

Soul Mate Relationships

When you are in a "Soul Mate" relationship the Child has no need to resurrect. You can make calm decisions and work through arguments. Movies have confused us so much. They have led us to believe that fighting equals passion, and heated fiery relationships signify true love. Soul Mates respect each other and want to see each other do well. When your Soul Mate hurts, you hurt, so when anxiety and fighting occurs you want to minimise it and go back to the calm bliss that true Soul Mates bring out in each other.

If you are interested in learning more about Cell Mates and Soul Mates, Katie has written something for all the Queens.

CELL MATES AND SOUL MATES - BY KATIE TODD

Shedding light on the true, often hidden and elusive dynamics within our significant relationships is life-changing.

Are we Cell Mates or Soul Mates in our various relationships? This question applies to all our relationships: with self, couples, family, friends, children and colleagues.

What is a Cell Mate?

To answer this question, we must explore our true relationship with ourselves. This is the most important relationship in our lives because it serves as the foundation and mirror to every other relationship we have.

Do you feel in any way entangled, stagnant, blocked, unhappy, lost, lonely, not good enough, too much or unfulfilled? That's what living in a Cell Mate relationship feels like.

If yes, you are living your life unconsciously locked in a painfully small gaol cell of fear-based reactions, beliefs and choices. This cell is created by our inner Child, who encapsulates our unique, childlike qualities. A Cell Mate life is having your inner Child of under five years of age ruling your life. That's like blindly letting your toddler drive your car and navigate your relationships and life decisions!

Our inner Child always makes self-sabotaging choices from hidden fears on autopilot, while we (the adults) are asleep at the wheel and absent. It's not a matter of if we will crash, but how soon and how big a crash will be.

When the Child within rules, we're living a Cell Mate survival existence.

Whenever we're stressed, rejected, blaming, shocked, unhappy, unwell, in crisis, triggered or reactive, we are in Child. Many so-called "chronological adults" have never developed an inner Adult. Many adults spend the majority of their lives operating reactively or passively from their Child. We insist on the worst-case scenario being the only possibility, would rather be right than happy, and are extremely black and white.

Unfortunately, external Soul Mate relationships cannot be found, created or nurtured from an inner Cell Mate relationship where our Child is running our life. When we are a Cell Mate within (i.e. without an adult in charge), we choose partners from a place of past lack and neediness, not compatibility.

Unveiling Childhood Family Dynamics with Personas

The unconscious blueprint for our lives and relationships is activated in our early years by our childhood family. We are all born with unique personalities (Personas) that contain specific strengths and weaknesses. My new language of ten Personas has been written specifically to help us better navigate Child Cell Mate relationships, so we can instead create and attract Adult Soul Mate partnerships. Personas also help us instantly recognise when we, or others, are in Child. This is invaluable, life-transforming information that helps our Adult assume the wheel of our lives.

The Ten Personas

Lion, Dog, Beaver, Swan, Raven, Owl, Peacock, Parrot, Nightingale and Sparrow.

The Personas are profound and complex, yet so accessible and relatable even children love and understand them. We each have a unique combination of Six Personas in varying strengths, and One key missing Persona we must develop to become whole – Adult.

Visit our official website www.personagrataprofiling.com to learn more about the Personas.

Cell Mate Painful Partnerships and "Family Replicas"

The family member who understood you least, or created the most conflict or unhappiness is almost guaranteed to be chosen (often repeatedly) as a significant partner figure at some stage in your life. These choices are unconscious Cell Mate choices from our Child. We compulsively choose parent or sibling replicas as partners/friends. We energetically recognise them from childhood. Whatever dynamic we wanted fixed as children therefore continues to drive our current choices, even though our childhood is long gone. We blindly seek an ideal "parent" or "sibling", not a partner, to heal our childhood lack and pain. This unconscious dynamic usually spells the beginning of the end, even before our relationship is off the ground.

"Family Replicas" are partners/people with very similar Personas to the original family member we felt least loved by. They do not share compatible Personas and values to ours. We are guaranteed 100% of the time to repeat the disastrously conflicted relationship dynamics of our childhood, when choosing a Family Replica.

We have all mistaken Persona familiarity, and our intense neediness to be seen and loved by the replica figure, as love. The Child will stubbornly refuse to leave the Family Replica, no matter how obviously toxic the relationship. The Child believes, if I can just get this Family Replica to love and appreciate me, I will become whole and loveable…

It never works.

Did we Choose a Cell Mate – Family Replica Partner?

Answer the following questions to find out.

Have you been feeling unhappy, stuck and lonely for some time in this relationship?

Are there topics that are "not allowed" to be discussed and that are therefore never resolved?

Do you often question this relationship and wonder if this is all there is?

How much of you (%) is celebrated and welcomed by your partner, how much is rejected and repressed?

Have you lost respect for your partner, and do you list their faults often?

Is there a history of unresolved painful events and resentment between you?

Do you walk on eggshells in this relationship, living in survival mode?

Do you have the same arguments repeatedly that get nowhere?

Does the relationship feel more like a power struggle than team partnership?

Is this the relationship you would wish for your children?

Now, going deeper...

Who was (or were) the family member(s) you had the most conflict or unhappiness with?

Exactly how did you feel with this person in childhood?

Do you feel a similar dynamic with your partner?

What were your key frustrations with the family member?

Are they present in your relationship today?

Is it possible when not communicating or connecting well, you're projecting your original family pain on top of the situation?

How often (%) have you and your partner been operating from Child lately?

Are you more a "brother/sister", "flatmate", "provider/ housekeeper" relationship or taking turns to be parent or child to each other?

Is there frequent passive-aggressive, withholding punishing behaviour or aggressive volatility present in your relationship?

Have you become the worst version of yourselves, and blame the other for your unhappiness?

Answering the questions above may indeed alert us to the fact that we are floundering. If we can see we have partnered a Family

Replica, then the first step is to realise it's reflecting one of our biggest issues. We must also stop projecting the original family member onto our partner. That's our baggage and it's unfair of us to add that onto them.

You stop attracting certain people when you heal the parts of you that once needed them.

Cell Mates	OR Soul Mates
Child in charge – shadow	Adult in charge – light
Unconscious	Conscious
Fear driven, blaming	Authentic, responsible
Takes things very personally	Sees all points of view
Lives a stagnant life	Lives a free and fulfilling life
Lives on autopilot reactively	Responsive, not reactive to life events
Seeks others to fulfil needs	Fulfils own needs
Repeats painful patterns endlessly	Embraces life as an opportunity to grow

Cell Mate relationships are ultimately deeply lonely experiences and very hard work.

The Five Kubler-Ross Stages of Grief: denial, anger, bargaining, depression and acceptance

In Cell Mate relationships, we have been living in one or more of the first four stages of grief. We may have battled long-term anger, denial, bargaining or depression in our relationships. We may also have seen the worst of ourselves on display, and living smaller, stagnant lives.

If you suspect you have been living with long-term grief, I strongly recommend seeking professional support.

Sacred Contracts

Every relationship is a Sacred Contract. The more significant the relationship, the bigger the contract, and more important the lessons.

The term "Sacred Contract" refers to a specific spiritual connection and agreement undertaken between souls, *before* we are born. On a soul level we plan, choose and design our key lessons we want to overcome with other souls, *in between* lifetimes. As we grow up, we are completely unconscious of these agreements initially, but if we do enough work, we come to see the underlying scripts at play in our lives.

The belief is, we've hit major roadblocks before in other lives, and consciously choose to have further practice with these tough lessons again this lifetime with particular people/souls, even though we know they will include great challenges.

Our issues/lessons can include worthiness, abandonment, trust, anger, selfishness, greed, timidity, laziness, patience, humility, courage, persistence, decisiveness and many others. *All* lessons are connected to our various expressions of fear, and are *our* specific blocks to love! The generic life lesson for humanity is to progressively free ourselves from our various blocks to love, over lifetimes.

We all have lessons we've chosen, whether aware of them or not. Our childhood *always* sets up perfect scenarios/actors to "trigger" our weak spots – key issues and lessons. We then walk into adulthood with invisible wounds and issues that keep tripping us up. From here we unconsciously choose partners (Cell Mates) who are guaranteed to continually trigger our key issues.

These relationships are Sacred Contracts. On an unconscious human level, we often don't appreciate this constant triggering, as they are our *most* painful relationships. However, in time we can gain the wisdom to realise their true purpose, to reflect how this issue operates *within* us.

In graduating from Cell Mate, Sacred Contract relationships, we finally graduate from the lesson we wrote for ourselves before we were born. Graduation requires that we *own* that we chose this experience/relationship on several levels, and that the dark issues the relationship reflected and triggered in us were indeed the entire point. They are *our* issues, it's not about hating and blaming "the other".

We have Cell Mate and Soul Mate Sacred Contracts in life. Most of us have to graduate from Cell Mate relationships first, before being mature enough to attract and create a Soul Mate relationship.

We know a Sacred Contract is fulfilled when we are able to graciously walk away from the ongoing drama. We recognise the painful dynamics as an ongoing reflection of our relationship with ourselves. We become neutral to "the other" and even grateful on a soul level.

We don't need to condone what's occurred, but we *must* see the part we played in creating the drama. When graduating from sacred contracts, we finally develop healthy boundaries and consciously choose *not* to set up or engage in these painful dances again on any level. Sacred Contracts are our most important and powerful teachers, if we can recognise their true purpose.

Soul Mate Relationship Qualities

Love is evident in actions, not just words.

There are many shared interests and values, and mutual love and respect.

Both feel innately safe and free to bring their entire self to the relationship.

Both are self-aware, emotionally honest and working on becoming more Adult.

Both are seen, heard, valued, respected and loved unconditionally.

Both learn not to take things personally, thereby avoiding unnecessary conflict.

Both recognise the specific Child behaviours and patterns in the other.

Both respect the differing strengths, interests, values and language of the other.

Both learn to hold themselves in Adult when the other slips into Child.

Both recognise the underlying fears and pain within each other's shadow.

Compassion is given when the other's Child pushes us away or goes into crisis.

Both fully commit to honest self-reflection, self-responsibility and growth.

Equal partnership, not power and control struggles from the Child.

Excellent communication skills, where both actively participate, listen and negotiate.

Both take full responsibility to meet their needs and express their opinions.

Neither expects the other to be a mind reader or perfect parent.

Both consistently self-parent, freeing the other to be partner, lover and friend.

It's a collaborative partnership that compels us to become more whole and be the best version of ourselves.

Most of the Child is expressed when out of our depth, or caught by surprise. Compassion in these moments transforms relationships.

Learning how to self-parent is the most essential ingredient to becoming an Adult Soul Mate and achieving contentment and happiness.

To create a Soul Mate partnership, we must first become a Soul Mate within.

If you would like to go further into "Who Am I? Cell Mate or Soul Mate", there are several things you can do. Visit our official website www.personagrataprofiling.com and complete the questionnaire to find out your exact Persona Profile. Then answer the quiz as if you are the family member you most struggled with, as well as past or present partners. This will reveal who did the actual choosing in your relationship – Child or Adult.

Your task is not to seek for Love, but merely to seek and find all the barriers within yourself that you have built against it.
– Rumi

Staying with a Family Replica

If you can clearly see a repeat of a painful childhood dynamic, it's time to have a deep and meaningful conversation with your partner. Ask how they are feeling in the relationship, what they would like to improve between you and where they hope you will both be in a few years' time. Have the courage to mention to each other, without blame, the aspects of the relationship that are not working. State what you both would like from your relationship and how you could practically rebuild and grow closer together. Changing old patterns and routines that keep you busy, disconnected or unavailable would be a great start.

Every time you are tempted to react in the same old way, ask if you want to be a prisoner of the past, or a pioneer of the future.
– Deepak Chopra

Lastly, the best advice I can offer is something I now live by in every type of relationship: Go where you are celebrated, not where you are merely tolerated.

– Katie Eden Todd

*

And that is exactly what I did. I found a place where I am celebrated. Too many women are accepting unhappiness as normality. Katie's approach isn't something new; we've all heard that we need to rely on ourselves first. I found happiness independent of a man – independent of anyone but myself – and then everything came together. If you find your place, the one where you're celebrated instead of just tolerated, run there. Unashamedly, fuck everyone's expectations of you, fuck right and fuck wrong. You didn't do the crime that warrants a Cell

Mate relationship because take it from me, a Soul Mate's love will change you. It's golden and it's all you need.

When we are in our Child we make foolish decisions, irrational ones, made from anger and fear. We can usually feel ourselves doing this, but struggle to control our inner child. Understandable; I struggle to control my actual children too.

We need to stop acting on our Child's emotions. It's OK to slip into "Child" and throw a little tantrum and act like a dick, but keep talking to a minimum and don't make big decisions. Kind of like taking Valium; you can make a cup of tea but don't drive a tractor.

When I was in my Child I found Javier, and believed he was right for me.

When I was in my Adult I found Denim, and have never felt more content. Now, I hope my Child doesn't chase him away!

Find the pain that gives your Child this repetitive behaviour and heal it. Be kind to it, show it that you're not going anywhere and that it's safe. You will never heal your inner Child by continually blaming and shaming it. Be understanding with yourself.

Or just bribe it to shut the fuck up. Maccas chips usually work for my kids.

FAT AND SKINNY WENT FOR A WALK. AND THEY NEVER CAME BACK BECAUSE YOU'RE ALL A BUNCH OF CUNTS

DENIM, THE PUB AND SOME DICK WHO MADE ME FEEL FAT

I didn't go out of my way to see Denim. A friend told me that she thought he had a crush on me, but I didn't really care. I bumped into him at the school while I was picking up my kids; he was with another mum, picking up her kids with her. He was a familiar face amongst a lot of mums that I didn't know. Ironically, I started a blog about the judgements that mums face and ended up being Australia's most judged mum – go figure.

I quickly sat with him. We chatted like old friends and he later told me that he was shocked I sat with him, but Denim is constantly underestimating how comforting he is.

I invited him to a gig I was going to with my brother and some friends that night. It was actually an old flame singing at our local pub but I didn't disclose that information. In fact, that was one of the reasons why I hadn't wanted to go but my brother insisted and it was from like twelve years ago, who cares?

The funny thing about getting ready to go out that night was that I couldn't decide what to wear. Whenever I'm feeling particularly uncomfortable with my weight, I struggle to find something to wear. I can try on every single thing I own – and I'm not gonna lie, I own a lot of clothes – and I'll find nothing I'm comfortable in. It's how I gauge my weight; I don't look at scales. But this was the first time since starting my body positive movement that I felt uncomfortable. Was single life going to do that to me? Bring back all of those insecurities around my body and appearance? Did I have the energy for that kind of uncertainty? Fuck knows.

I opted for tight jeans and a baggy red singlet made from the type of fabric that gives away every detail of my boobs and nipples without actually being see-through. I had massive saggy boobs for most of my life. They grew saggy and everyone said, "Enjoy your tits coz they only grow down from here," and it freaked me out coz my tits had nowhere to go. They were already down – there were no backless tops or bra-less dresses, ever. Then the babies came. I basically lived in maternity bras and tight singlets over the top of them. I was always quite slim when I was younger so it was a bit of a shame to have to strap up like I did, but they were size double F. They sat around my belly button, completely hiding my figure. So, when I was 28 years old, I had them reduced and lifted.

It was one of the best things I have ever done. A close friend of mine had implants put in at around the same time of my reduction, and she described similar feelings to what I experienced when mine were reduced – freedom and self-love; all the things that people want us to believe don't come from plastic surgery.

I used to judge plastic surgery, but after having my breasts reduced, I'm all for it. If something is weighing you down and you can change it, change it; if you don't want to change it, don't, but try to change your mindset. Each to their own. Who are we to decide what a healthy mindset is? Everyone is so different.

Since having my breasts reduced and lifted, I have been in love with them, and often find myself dismissing life's problems with, "at least I have good tits," and that's exactly what I said to myself the night that I walked out of my house for the gig. I may have struggled immensely to get my jeans buttoned up, and to find a singlet baggy enough to not snuggle up to my muffin top, and I may not be able to sit down properly all night… but at least I had good tits.

I got there before Denim. I was sitting with my brother and his mates, a group of nineteen-year-olds comparing dick stories:

"I think I've got drip dick."

"Well, then we all have drip dick, we've been fucking the same chicks."

"What's drip dick?"

"It's when your dick oozes but you haven't figured out what STD you have."

I didn't know if they were joking or not, but I knew that drip dick didn't make me excited to be single.

Denim walked in; he looked different than usual, like he'd washed his hair or something: he was wearing a fitted light blue top, jeans and black boots.

In other words: he wants me.

I hadn't seen him in boots before. In fact, that might have been the first time I saw him in shoes. There were no seats with me, so he sat with a friend of mine, and I went over and gave him a hug hello and we spoke for a while; Denim and I talk so effortlessly.

We discussed my career. He knew more about me then he had originally let on, referencing times that I had been interviewed and different posts that I had written.

Later that night, while I was watching the musician that I used to shag sing, I turned around to get a drink and saw one of my brother's friends.

He said to me, "Hey, I was looking through your Instagram today. Fuck, you used to be so hot!"

I was a bit taken aback. "Sorry?"

"Like, when you were younger, even after you had Billie-Violet and Arlo, but the twins, they really fucked your body. I can't believe how hot you used to be."

My heart skipped a beat. I usually wouldn't let something like that fuck up my night, but I was feeling particularly sensitive, particularly not myself, and everything just stood still. I couldn't shake his words. I told him that I thought he was really rude, that it was obviously going to hurt my feelings and he responded with, "I can talk about it though, coz this is what you blog about, you know it and you write about it so I can say that, yeah? Coz I mean, you were a really attractive woman and I can't believe what the twins did to your body."

The truth is that the twins never fucked my body. A number of things contributed to the fact that I am now ten kilos heavier then I have ever been, one of those things being that writing uses so much less physical energy than hairdressing.

And the answer is NO. Just because I can say it doesn't mean you can. When I say it, I'm empowering myself; when you say it, you're stepping over a line. It was like he was excited to finally be able to call a chick fat, because she said it first. Even my brother, who's insensitive at the best of times, was shaking his head.

And that was my night done. Would you believe that even me, body positive me with over a million followers who love their bodies just that tiny bit more because of how much I appreciate mine, found herself crying in the toilets that night? Not even great tits could snap me out of it.

Denim noticed I wasn't right. He bought me a drink, and while everyone was getting pretty pissed and I saw my opportunity to slip away, Denim noticed and he offered to walk my friend and me home. She thought it was a great idea, but I didn't. I kissed him on the cheek and snapped that we were going home alone.

I needed to lick my wounds; my mate gave me "Queens' Counselling" on the walk home. I wanted to believe her that I was beautiful and powerful and could lose weight if I wanted to, but no matter what was said, I was still left feeling pretty shit.

I decided that I needed to lose a few kilos. I wasn't going to blog about it because it felt contradictory to everything I always say. I could claim it was for health reasons, I could say it was out of stress. But the truth was, I just wanted to feel a bit slimmer and if that made me a fraud, so be it.

Eating disorders and body image disappointment will stay with you for a lifetime.

Anybody who triggers the related anxieties needs to either be told to shut the fuck up, or be excused from your life. Sometimes it's a family member, sometimes it's a dickhead from the pub. Be gone, Fuckbrain.

KIDS AND BODY IMAGE - BEATING THE ODDS

The thing about body image, eating disorders and low self-esteem is that they can punch you in the face when you least expect them to.

I went from being a chubby teenager, who was teased about her weight nonstop and hated herself, to a chubby bulimic teenager, who hated herself just as much and couldn't figure how her body didn't reflect her eating disorder, to a nervous wreck of a young adult who basically ate nothing and was constantly told how beautiful she looked and was finally accepted by all the boys and girls. Accepted into the "secret world of skinny", whose doors had been well and truly shut all these years.

Only I still hated myself, so much so that I remember sitting on the couch at the bar I worked at, so angry at myself for picking some cheese and pineapple off a piece of pizza and eating it that I was actually scratching chunks of skin off my ankle under the table as punishment – something to look at the next time I dared to think about eating again. I've never told anyone that. It feels strange to even put it to paper; funny how we can behave in a way that appears so out of control as a means of gaining control.

Then to a pregnant woman who could literally not stop the weight gain. All I had to look forward to was food: packet chips, drive-through, ice cream. Even now I'm cracking a slippery just thinking about how much fun I had getting fat.

To a stressed mother who cared more about losing baby weight than sleeping patterns or my own sanity, and back to a chubby woman who hates herself… and so on. It's a wheel, and just like the little mouse on his wheel trying to get the cheese, it's exhausting.

Overeating and undereating are just as dangerous and depressing as each other. In fact, I often think a lot more concern is placed on the undereater, while the emotional overeater is just as depressed.

I have a theory that this is why overweight people can be so defensive. When I was underweight, people were coming to me with concern, "Are you sure you're OK? We are all a bit worried that you don't eat." Boys called me cute, thought my small appetite made me desirable and low maintenance, but when I was overweight, I became a joke: "Be careful *Sea Shepherd* doesn't come to your rescue when you sunbake." And those who don't directly turn you into a joke are doing it behind your back. People laugh at fat people. It's that simple.

I was abused and called a fat cow. Once when I was sober and picking up friends from the pub, a man told me that I was a fat bitch who didn't belong there, as one of his friends failed to hold in his laughter and spat out his beer.

Nobody seems to take into consideration the turmoil and heartache that goes on inside an emotional overeater's mind when they are in bed at night. Never, not when I was bulimic, nor when I was underweight, was I as unhappy as when I felt like I had no control over my eating. And the only thing I can compare it to, the only thing that makes sense to me, is addiction. When someone talks about drug addiction, something I've been lucky enough to not be affected by, I can relate with my overeating.

I made a promise to myself every night that tomorrow I'd be better, tomorrow is a new day and I wasn't going to eat carbs, or the really ambitious: I'm not eating anything, a juice detox or a fast, or... whatever the new words are that make you sound healthy and of a balanced mind.

But the truth is that when you're hungry, you fuck up. You eat carbs for brekkie and you might as well make a day of it, which turns into a week of it, and while you're ordering another cheeseburger for your kid (who doesn't eat cheeseburgers) you know it isn't a cheat meal, it's a cheat life, and before you know it you utterly hate yourself again. You can't get comfortable in bed because every position you lie in, you can feel your full, round stomach, which makes you despise your fat pig self for having no self-control, and the only way to cope is to make those promises to yourself again. "Tomorrow, the juice cleanse starts."

You blame everything on your weight – you would have got that job if you weren't fat, you'd have a boyfriend if you weren't fat, even the cat doesn't let you hug her because you're fucking fat. Your behaviour resembles that of someone who doesn't belong here, that of someone who has no right to be here. In return, people start to treat you as if you don't. You hide your body while sleeping with a man. He will pick up on your self-loathing and not call you back, confirming once again that you are a fat pig who doesn't deserve love.

But, oh yes, continue to only worry about the underweight women, and don't forget to make another joke about the overweight ones.

I can't pinpoint any particular occasion that gave me an eating complex, a food complex, a weight complex. But having recently spoken to some experts in the field, I feel a little wiser on the subject, along with an explanation for why it affects so many of us.

You see, it comes from an early age. We develop our idea of what is perfect and so many things contribute to that idea: TV, magazines, our parents and, of course, now we have social media. So imagine you are around six years old, all of the TV presenters look a certain way. I used to call it the "Kookai" way – have you ever tried to look good in Kookai when you're a few kilos overweight? Fuck my life, it hides nothing. All of the models look a certain way, and you start to believe that to be successful, you too must look that way.

And you take on other people's opinions. "She is so hot, look at that billboard, I wanna look like that." (*Life will be better if I grow up to be tall and really skinny*).

A mother or sister: "I have nothing to wear, I look so fat." (*Better not get fat because clothes won't fit you and your mum won't think you look nice*).

And that charming Uncle: "Jesus, Con, you're getting a bit of a belly there, what have you been eating?" (*Oh my God, it's starting. I eat too much and nobody will love me or let me succeed*).

I am not exaggerating. All of these things and many more happened to me and I, in turn, interpreted even worse. Then I hit my teenage years and it became so much more damaging.

I can remember every single time a family member body-shamed me. Do you know why? Because you feel shame so intensely, you don't forget that shit and you do what you have to do to avoid feeling it again.

After children, it was time. Time to shed the ideals, and time to value myself as something other than the number on the scales, or the number on the back of my jeans. Aren't we worth more than numbers?

I realised that I was a mother. I needed to be a role model, not just to them but to myself too. I realised what everyone of a certain age and wisdom has tried to tell me all along: "Your looks will fade, my dear," and they will, and the people who relied solely on them will be left behind.

That's when I embarked on my self-acceptance journey. I think it will always be a journey, I don't know if there is a destination. It is so much easier said than done. Tired of always changing my body to look hot, I thought it was time to change my definition of hot, to my body. A brilliant theory.

Only, when have you have lifelong memories of depression associated with weight gain, and of freedom associated with weight loss, you are talking about some huge belief systems to break through.

I made an effort to change the voices in my head. A lot of that was done with the spoken word: "fat bitch" turned into "sexy bitch". I watched the way I spoke about other women, as that was often a reflection of the way that I saw myself. I would happily buy a size large if that was the most comfortable size and I was even at a point where I could lose a bit of weight to keep my health in check, without taking it to extreme levels.

Then I met Denim.

Overeating and undereating should be looked at with the same severity.

You are not invisible no matter what size or shape you are. It is not you who must speak louder; it is the world around you that must be taught to listen properly.

Repeat after me, "I am a sexy bad arse bitch. My body is a very clever, sexual temple and I'm a good dancer. One day I'll be dead, but I'll be happy because I ate cake and made a lot of people jealous."

DENZY AIN'T SO PERFECT AFTER ALL

You see, Denzy has absolutely no idea what it's like to feel insecure about the way he looks. Sure, he thinks his nose is too big but, in general, he has never felt bad about himself or felt disappointed with his weight. So many men don't. They grow up with other pressures: being a man, providing, being successful, but the emphasis is never on doing it all with six-pack, a quiff and a sparkling smile.

Denim has no body fat and he eats everything. He doesn't need to exercise. Sure, he surfs, but when I met him he had been sick and hadn't surfed for a whole year, while still rocking a six-pack. It's genetics; his son has the same body. The first time I saw Denzy without a shirt on, I took a deep breath in and immediately saw all of my jiggling rolls look up at me and laugh, "Where is all that body confidence now? Coz we ain't going anywhere, biatch."

You see, I never go for lean or fit guys and I had always ended up with guys who were a bit more natural looking, a bit softer, probably because the idea of a guy going to the gym really turns me off. I suppose that's because I don't want to go to the gym, because I like the couch and Maltesers. I wasn't going to hold it against the poor guy. He's hot; he can't help it. I'm sure the universe didn't make him hot as a way of getting back at me; it's just a side effect.

The problem was that, in my mind, that meant that he wouldn't understand my body and I didn't really feel like flaunting it in front of his skin, muscle and bone combination.

I gained ten kilos last year, as soon as my blog took off and the media started writing about me. I tried to figure out why fame made me fat when it made everyone else thin, but I couldn't figure it out. Was it stress? Was it happiness? I ended up kind of putting it down to "business" – I don't walk to the shops because I have too many emails to reply to, I buy much more food than I used to because any minute I can save is a minute that I can catch up on some work, and if I do get free time I like to spend it with the kids (who would love a walk or bike ride but whatevs, that doesn't align with my self-excuses).

So now that fame has made me fat and I met the perfect Denzy, I was losing confidence in myself. It took a few weeks for me to shake the feeling, for me to remember all of the things that I had trained myself to believe. Denim had made a few comments that led me to believe he was usually into slim chicks. He even compared me to one, one night, and I won't forget the words. He said, "She has a hot body, but she is fucked in the head, sure you don't have her body, but you're sexy inside and out."

Of course, that may be perfectly fine for someone who hasn't judged herself for twenty years on how her body looked, for someone who hasn't spent so long in the toilets determined to spew up a meal that her body will absolutely not let go of, her entire face is swollen. But to me? All I heard was, "You're fat and you'll never be hot like her, sure you've got a good 'personality', but ain't nobody drooling over character."

I let it go. Well, when I say "I let it go", I mean I didn't dump him, but I bring it up all the time; if he even looks at me while I'm eating, he is likely to hear, "You don't have a good body and blah, blah, fucking blah," as bits of food fall out of my mouth and land on my tummy and tits.

Denim and I had got to a point where we were comfortable with each other's bodies, so much so that his body blurred into mine. We slept in a tangled mess. He learnt about the struggles I'd had with body image and reassured me that I was changing what he found sexy; he hadn't been with a woman my size and now found himself checking out all kinds of curvy chicks. I loved that, I loved that he was changing his ideas of sexy. I realised that I didn't want to look slim, I wanted to look sexy and if I could look sexy to him as I am, why would I want to change?

Until one day.

We were in London, staying in an Airbnb while I was touring. Denim was out with the kids at a skate park and I was home early, getting ready to go to dinner with the founder of Rafiki, the charity I work with, when I saw it.

Denim's phone.

I don't know what came over me, a spill over of mistrust from previous relationships, fears and insecurities, or outright selfishness that lead me to picking up his phone. Denim doesn't cheat. It's one of the reasons I married him; I can't stand dishonesty, cheating or disloyalty. Denim understands the meaning of a team and that's what we are.

So why then go through his phone? I don't know. Because I'm a fuckhead?

There wasn't much juice in there. Denzy literally lives for his kids so it was just a whole lot of:

How are the kids?

and:

Where will the boys skate this weekend?

and so on. So out of complete idiocy, I decided to see what Denim was saying about me to his friends. It has always intrigued me, as I was the one who chased him.

I saw a message thread between him and his best friend and I scrolled up, I scrolled to around the time that we met and read a message from his mate:

So did you think this Constance chick wants it? ("It" must have been what Denim considers his dick of diamonds).

He'd responded:

Yeah probably, but she's not my type, too chunky for me.

And my heart broke. Into a million pieces. I cried and hated myself. But do you know what? I hated Denim more. For having the smallest mind in the world, for not being worthy of my time and for being so superficial that he would sleep with a skinnier woman just because she was fucking skinnier.

Do you know what? I just got a migraine even remembering that night. I was so crushed.

Denim returned home, walked into the room and straight away saw on my face that shit was going down.

"What is it?" I'll never forget the fear in his eyes.

"I went through your phone."

And his face scrunched up, still unsure of what exactly I had seen, (which still, to this day, makes me wonder what the fuck else was in there) and he yelled, "Why did you do that?"

"Don't turn this around on me. You're the one bragging to your mates that I wanted to fuck you, but I'm too chunky for fucking you."

And he just sat there, head in his hands, while I lashed out. "What is wrong with you? How could I be so stupid? Why would you humiliate me like that to your friends?"

And, finally, his excuse. "I'm sorry, I hadn't seen you naked. I hadn't slept with you, all I had to go by was all of the things you put online, you in your undies on the couch balancing a beer on your belly. (Legend.) It was such a stupid thing to say. I feel like I've learnt so much about you and about women since I've been with you, everything has changed, and of course I think you're sexy, we have the best sex life."

I couldn't forgive him, I felt so ashamed. It cut me so deeply. He asked me if he could still come to dinner with the charity that evening.

"No. No way. I am meeting with a woman who has given up her entire life to care for sexually abused children in Kenya. I am talking about the people who are changing this world, do you hear me? World changers, saving children's lives! People I aspire to be like, my idols. You are just an insignificant little boy who talks about women's bodies to his friends, you do not get to sit at a table with this woman."

And proud as fuck of that speech, I walked downstairs, only to be followed three minutes later by Denim, who was not taking no for an answer.

"That's not fair, I respect you so much. I respect Rafiki, meeting the founder was one of the things I was looking forward to the most on this trip, you have to let me come." So I did, but I sat in the back of the car, couldn't talk to him or look at him all night.

Funnily enough, while I was in the back of the car I took a selfie, partly to make myself feel better and partly because I had put so much makeup on as payback to Denim that I was interested in how it translated on my camera with a filter. Months later, I would post that selfie when I needed a picture for a blog and all of the comments revolved around how sad my eyes looked.

When we got there, I couldn't help myself, When I'm in crisis, which is most days, I overshare; I tell shop assistants more then they want to know, I literally grab anyone and blurt out my current state of affairs.

Anne Marie Tipper is the founder of Rafiki Mwema; she is a blonde-haired, curvaceous and beautiful woman in her fifties with the warmest smile you'll ever come across. Everyone who meets her wants to be adopted by her, which is ironic considering she has around seventy foster children in Kenya. She is a child therapist and specialises in trauma.

To say I was traumatised by Denim's comments might be slightly dramatic, but I was highly pissed off. Anne Marie, glowing and beaming with her usual kindness, was telling me how much she liked Denim and how happy for me she was. I couldn't help myself and I blurted out what had just happened. I don't think I was doing it to make her angry at Denim, I was doing it in the hope of making myself feel better. And she didn't hate Denim at all, she (annoyingly) took no interest into his stupid comments whatsoever and said to me, "Con, have you ever thought that you don't believe you deserve to be happy? You had to really search for that. It almost sounds to me like you are purposely sabotaging your own happiness."

She was right. I was. I always have. I'm not comfortable with happy. I almost felt relieved when I found that message, like I could finally go back to being miserable and not living with a fear that this is all a facade. Denim couldn't fix this; I needed to fix it.

And, needless to say, I eventually forgave him. I believe him, he treats me with such respect and kindness, he's always telling people and me how beautiful I am; I feel beautiful, you'd have to be on crack to not see how hot I am, for fuck's sake.

But it's there; it's always there. Self-doubt, food guilt. Learning to live with it has been, and possibly will always be, my biggest hurdle.

My daughter asked me if she was chubby recently.

I was baffled. Where on earth did she get that idea?

She told me that the girls at her school have been telling her that they think they are chubby and now she's wondering if she is.

I remembered a time when I was 16, angry at myself for not having the strength to go hungry for the greater good of my figure. One night I was at the markets having dinner with a friend and her family.

Her dad's friend didn't like me. I could feel it, even though I had only met him a couple of times. I was eating fried rice and he started to tell me that I was gaining weight.

He wanted to hurt me, it was obvious.

He said, "Every time I see you, you are bigger and now that I have seen you shove that plate of rice into your mouth so fast I can understand why."

I wish those words didn't affect me. I wish they didn't make me loathe myself and question the right that a pig like me had to even sit at the same table as normal people. But they did.

And now as a mum, I would do anything in my goddamn human fucking powers to protect my babies from EVER feeling like that.

The truth is, there was only one pig at that table and that pig broke a young girl's heart.

Now as a woman I have friends, friends that tell me all the time how gorgeous I am, how beautiful they are, how divine the stranger crossing the fucking road is and I believe it.

Just like these little girls questioning themselves makes my girl question herself, fear breeds fear, love breeds love.

I don't have the answers for raising a Queen who loves her body in whatever form it is. But I can encourage her to breed that kind of self-love.

So I told her that her body is perfect, I told her that my body is perfect, I told her that sometimes girls question themselves, so how about instead of letting that make you question yourself you just give them a great big hug and tell them that they are perfect too.

She smiled and ran off. She hasn't mentioned the word chubby again, so I may have actually had a parenting win.

Con x

Don't sabotage your own unhappiness, even if DRAMA and betrayal are your normal. It's never too late to redefine your normal.

Just because a bloke acts like a superficial cockhead, doesn't mean he is one. We all say cockhead things.

Don't go looking for things you don't want to find. Except head lice, still gotta look for them.

THE SLAP IN THE FACE
WE ALL NEED

Over a year ago, I met Lisa Magill.

She wrote a blog called *Terminally Fabulous* and she and I hit it off instantly. Lisa was a tiny woman with a mammoth personality; she was bossy and dominating and came from such a beautiful place that you almost wanted to be told what to do by her.

Lisa overshared in a way that even put me to shame; it was part of her charm. Watching her make people squirm by being too truthful for this world was one of my favourite things about her. I suppose that's why her blog was so successful.

She would write about her diagnosis and I learnt that the journey of a terminal patient isn't just the one diagnosis and coming to terms with it. It's about the hope – sometimes they feel like they aren't dying and sometimes they are diagnosed all over again when test results don't go their way. I feel like it's a downhill journey with plateaus along the way, plateaus that make you feel like you're back on solid ground.

The thing I loved about Lisa was how open she was about her fear; there was never a point where Lisa said, "If I get here... I don't want to continue" or, "Don't let me be in 'x' amount of pain, I'd rather be at peace."

So many people are so brave with dying, especially towards the end. I related so much to Lisa's will to live, probably because I'm a big fucking pussy who never wants to die.

Lisa did not mince her words; she did not want to die.

And why should she have to? Lisa was 34, why should she want to do anything but fight?

Her body went from a tiny little fit woman with a pixie haircut who looked ace in a string bikini, to having her body thrown around so much from her medicine that she told me she did not recognise the bloated woman in the mirror, to telling me that the new medicine that could possibly give her a few more months was giving her a buffalo hump.

Did any of that ever make Lisa think about stopping? About giving up? Of course not.

Lisa wanted this body to keep her around. She wanted this body to drag her soul through another day, she wanted this body even if it was blasted, if it was in a wheelchair; she just wanted this body to keep her here, with the people she loved – her mum Geraldine, her dad Peter, her brother and sister-in-law and their daughter Ava, who felt like more than a niece to Lisa. She just wanted to be here, to have just another day, or another week, to spend with the people that she loved.

While Lisa loved to talk about dying and opened the curtain on this taboo, she wasn't comfortable talking about her own death. It was just too painful, too unbearable, and up until the very last minute, Lisa believed something would save her. This just couldn't happen, she hadn't even had kids yet; she was so young, too young. She loved her family so much and she had the dreaded fear that one day, they would forget her.

Lisa Magill deserves to be here today but on March 11, 2017 she lay in the hospital, just skin and bones, and the cancer that had taken everything except her soul finally took her life.

My favourite memory of Lisa is dancing with my best friend, Annaliese, at a Rafiki fundraiser. It was late, everyone was drunk, and she turned to the small crowd of her family and friends and shouted, "HOW GOOD IS LIFE?"

So… how good is it? How good are those smiles on your kid's chubby little cheeks? How good is a big cuddle from your man when he's finally finished work for the week? How good does it feel when the kids finally break for Christmas and you know that you get to see the whole family?

I've learnt a lot lately. I've spoken to a lot of women and a lot of specialists and I've learnt that life is about our connections, about our love. This is the meaning of human existence, this is the reason we are here and the reason we don't want to leave; it's not death we are scared of, it's losing the ones we love.

And with all this beauty, with all this love, with your little boy who comes in to be cuddled at 3am because he's scared, or your little girl who sits on the kitchen bench and chats to you while you peel potatoes… who the fuck are you to be unhappy with your body? Who the fuck am I to hate myself because I'm not thin? That is the most absurd notion I have ever heard of.

We aren't here forever. Only the luckiest of us are still here.

I feel lucky.

I'm not saying I have the answers. I still eat too much and try to counteract it by eating nothing (which I never succeed at) but every day, I will do my best to honour this smoking hot bitch of a sexy, curvaceous goddess body that's keeping me here, that's facilitating all of the love we feel for everyone every day.

For my darling Lisa, you needn't fear every being forgotten.

Imagine looking back when you're eighty and calculating how many years you spent unhappy with yourself because of the way your body looked. Now imagine your daughter doing the same? It's time, time to stop. Time to live.

We are here only once and could be gone tomorrow. Every minute you spend wishing you looked a different way is a minute you're taking away from loving those dearest to you.

SOME SIMPLE AND PRACTICAL ADVICE FROM A PROFESSIONAL

I was going to leave you with my own personal experience with an eating disorder and negative body image. But on reflection, I feel this is such an important matter, affecting both our own and our children's lives, that I've sought some advice from a professional in the field, Dani Rowlands. Dani works at The Butterfly Foundation, a wonderful Australian organisation that supports people with eating disorders and body image issues.

DANI ROWLANDS

The relationship we have with our body is often one of the most complex and challenging of all relationships experienced. Our body image is made up of the thoughts, feelings and attitudes we have about our body and how we look, but it is not static. Our body image is influenced by many things: developmental changes, people, events and, of course, our ever-pervasive society that values appearance above other attributes. Given our culture's obsession with perfection and beauty and its fear of "fat", it is no wonder negative body image is a very real mental health problem for so many people.

Studies report that children as young as four are displaying a strong weight bias, and it has become far too common to hear children and teens voice body insecurities and feel dissatisfied with how they look. It is concerning the number of young people who are subjected to appearance-based bullying and teasing, and heartbreaking to see the growing number of children and adolescents requiring support for mental health problems and mental illnesses.

So, what can we do to support the development of a healthy body image in our children and challenge our image-obsessed culture at the same time?

Show them what a healthy body image looks like. Nothing is more impactful than seeing something in action. There will be days when we feel uncomfortable in our skin, but it's what you do during those times; how you speak to your body and what behaviours you engage in that count most. Speaking kindly to and about our bodies, and those of others, is important. Help your children to sit comfortably during times of body discomfort to build their resilience.

Give yourself permission to heal. No one is ever too old to start healing their relationship with their body, or with food. It might be something you feel you can manage alone, or if more serious issues or an eating disorder have not been supported or treated, professional support will be required. Everyone deserves to feel at peace with, and in, their body.

Mind your language! Appearance talk – for example fit, fat, thin, muscles, healthy, ageing, wrinkles, and so on – may give you a platform to disclose body insecurities, but it's far from helpful in the long run and it does not improve body satisfaction. Appearance talk has been normalised and it unfortunately only serves to reaffirm the ideal that thinness, muscularity and youthfulness are better; more desirable, successful and lovable. Do your best to disengage from this talk whenever you can and help your children to do the same. The more we strive for perfection and talk about perfect looks, the more important these things become.

Discourage dieting and extreme exercise behaviours. If nothing else, do not encourage your child or teen to diet or restrict food. Ever! And ideally, they wouldn't witness dieting or extreme/rigid exercise in their home either. Dieting behaviours can disorder a person's relationship with food (also known as disordered eating) and this can be detrimental to a young person's physical development and mental health. Dieting in children and adolescents is considered risky behaviour and is a significant risk factor for the development of eating disorders.

"Healthy" is not a one-size-fits-all. Our health is determined by so much more than just our body weight. Children and adults can be healthy at a higher weight and we cannot always tell by looking at someone what their health status is. It is important to accept your child's developing body, so that they can do the same. A body is not "wrong" if it doesn't fit the societal beauty ideal. As a parent, this message is a vital one to reinforce.

If you are concerned about your child's health or physical development, seek advice from a health professional – and ideally, they would not encourage restrictive dieting, so seek out the support from a non-diet health professional!

Encourage your child to move, nourish and nurture their body. With so many conflicting health messages it's easy to see why people are confused. The language we use and what we demonstrate when it comes to food and exercise can help to foster healthy behaviours in our children.

- Encourage non-competitive movement, for yourself and your child. Use positive motivators such as mental health, functionality, wellbeing and enjoyment over weight loss or body shape change. Discourage using food as a motivator to move.

- Support the development of a positive relationship with food. There is an abundance of information on what children "should" eat, and it's of course important to offer a variety of nutritious foods and not demonise "sometimes" foods; however it is equally important to teach children how to eat, allowing their body to be their guide. Help children to listen to their body and recognise their signs of hunger, satiety and fullness (this is known as intuitive eating) and also to eat mindfully, so they eat slowly and with their senses. It's important to use language that does not promote our harmful diet culture, or demonise or shame food or food groups. Food is fuel for life and is allowed to be enjoyed; it is not, and need not be, a tool to punish or soothe ourselves with.

- Help your child to find positive tools to manage their stressors and negative emotions. What works for each of us will be different and change over time. Using strategies that don't involve food or intense exercise is key: music, art, writing, gentle exercise, breathing and mindfulness exercises are all great activities that can support them in a really helpful way.

Savvy on social media. Research continues to confirm the negative impact that social media has on self-esteem and body confidence. It has become a platform that facilitates unfair body comparisons.

- Talk to your child about how what they see may not always be real! Cropping, filters and editing tools create the illusion of perfection, just like in the media. We never truly know what is happening in real time, behind the image.

- Empower your child to be aware of how they feel when using social media. Do certain images and people make them feel inspired or triggered? If they are criticising and comparing themselves or feeling the need to compensate with their behaviours to compete with what they see, a social media cleanse (or a break) is required.

- Block or unfollow people and pages that promote "#thinspo" and "#fitspo" messages, and those that endorse our toxic diet culture. Teach your child how to report people, pages and comments that incite hate.

- If your child is objectifying or sexualising themselves on their pages, it's important to find a way to talk with them about it. Enquire and seek to understand – without judgement.

Listen and acknowledge. Knowing what to say in the moment when your child talks negatively about their body can be tough. Statements such as "I feel fat", or "I'm so ugly" can be a way to voice their body insecurities or flag that something else is going on. Take a breath first before responding. Listen attentively, and don't dismiss what they say as not important. You don't have to fix it for them but you can empathise: *"I have days like that too"* or *"I'm sorry you feel that way"*. Sharing experiences you had when you were their age often helps them relate to you in that moment and they may feel more comfortable to talk.

Fat is not a feeling! It is also not bad or something to fear, so it can also be a good time to challenge weight stigma (perhaps when a teen has calmed down!)

Rather than assuring them that they look beautiful, thin etc., remind them that their body IS great.

If these comments are becoming more frequent and your child is becoming preoccupied with their body, food and/or exercise we encourage you to speak to a health professional.

If concerned, seek help sooner than later. It is estimated that one in 24 Australians are experiencing an eating disorder. Eating disorders are serious and complex mental and physical illnesses and they develop for a range of reasons, affecting males and females of all ages. Parenting styles are not to blame and despite best efforts, serious body image issues and eating disorders can and do develop.

If you are concerned that your child is experiencing something more serious than body dissatisfaction, trust your instincts. Seeking support sooner rather than later can reduce the severity and duration of eating disorders and make a full recovery more likely.

*

As children develop and grow, we're not always going to say the right thing or respond in the right way. And that is OK. We can only do our best in each moment and resource ourselves with knowledge and skills so we can improve with each interaction.

Strive to speak and be kind to yourself and your body and do all you can to not let your worth be dictated by what you weigh or how you look. Be more than your body!

While body image is influenced by many things, parents can be one of the most significant and positive influences on their child's, and that is exciting!

Butterfly's National Helpline 1800 ED HOPE is a free and confidential service, providing eating disorder and negative body image support and referral via phone, web chat and email. It is available to all Australians, 8am-12am, Mon-Sun.

1800 33 4673 (1800 ED HOPE) or

www.thebutterflyfoundation.org.au

ONLINE BULLYING

THE FIRST LOVE STORY THAT DIDN'T BEGIN WITH LOVE

I didn't see Denim again for quite a while. He made no effort and neither did I, and I wasn't exactly interested in fucking my head around just as it was gaining clarity.

At that time in my life, something inside me stopped caring, like my heart turned off. Too much pain and disappointment clouded my vision for seeing anyone for what they were.

As my counsellor said, "You are like a racehorse, but you never rest, you just go around, and around, and around. Something will force you to stop one day."

I suppose when love and life hurts you, and hurts you, and hurts you, your heart makes the decision without your head – you just can't care anymore. I remember feeling that shift, that my heart had let go of love. It wasn't broken, it had just been broken so many times that it could no longer break anymore.

I often think that my heart broke for the final time when my dad died. He was my everything. He taught me everything I know and loved me with every inch of himself. His bright blue eyes smiled at me every time they saw me. Even when he was in pain, he smiled at me, he laughed at all of my jokes, bragged about me to his family, told me that no man deserved a woman like me.

Losing him was losing a part of myself. I built a barrier. I'd never let a man hurt me, nobody deserved to. Nobody would ever mean as much to me as he did. There was no need to mend this broken heart, it will serve me so much more broken.

I wasn't about to go out of my way and chase Denim, but I still had to write the post about the time that I met him, about the fact that he yanked his kids out of school after his ex-wife had died and drove them around the country, about how gorgeous his children are. And I did it and it went crazy. 130k likes on the post and a reach of around four million.

It seems that I wasn't the only person that Denim resonated with.

A couple of weeks ago after taking the kids out for dinner, I grabbed a couple of beers and went to the skate park to tire them out so they crash without fighting.

There were two kids there, long blonde-haired kids whose skating skills defied the laws of gravity and who spoke kindly and respectfully to the younger, less talented kids like mine.

And I met Denim, their dad.

He had long hair and an obvious story to tell, and we started chatting.

I was intrigued by these children, while my son complains that he needs his fortieth pair of shoes for the month and is picking his nose in front of the school principal, these guys are winning state competitions, training younger kids and have an incredible ability to connect with adults.

They must have a mum with her shit way more together then me.

Their dad must be totally strict and focused...

Well, that night I learnt that these children were pulled out of school against all advice, without even homeschooling, and driven around Australia on a quest to skate every single skate park in the country.

You see, a few years ago, Denim had the horrific job of telling these two gorgeous boys that their mum had died by suicide.

After that period of indescribable hardship, Denim decided they need to pick up and leave, giving away or throwing away all of his possessions and embarking on a trip of healing. With no timeframe or certain direction, he told me that he let his children "choose their day" – if they saw something they wanted to do, they just did it.

Schools said no, they said the boys would be held down a year, police even pulled him over, questioning why the kids weren't at school. But Denim followed his parenting instincts and gave the boys what they needed to heal.

All on a modest single parent's pension, which we all know couldn't have been easy.

They decided to hold their heads high and made a pact to make their mum proud and speak of her only in the light and never dwell on the darkness.

Upon returning, Denim asked the schools for one request, don't hold them down. They have grown and healed a lot, please just let them try in their own year levels.

The school agreed and what do you know? They flew through the year.

Not to mention the boys both won "king of the concrete" 1st and 2nd in the state and have 3–4 sponsors each.

Pretty fucking rad for high school kids.

It just reinforces my belief that everyone's doing what they believe their kids need and sometimes the most unconventional parenting turns out to be the most beneficial.

Proud to know these kids and call Denim a new friend.

 Total King

The post was heavily monitored; whenever I write about someone else, I have many admins monitor the page and hide rude, aggressive responses or any comments with a negative sentiment, simply because I am borrowing someone else's story and I know how terrible it can feel to have horrible things said about you. Why should I subject someone else to that?

People often accuse me of deleting mean comments, or comments by people who disagree with me. The truth is that I delete comments that start comment-section wars. That's the one thing I hate about the internet – the passive-aggressive comment-section wars. Someone says something kind of derogatory towards me, and one of the Queens will come in to bat, before you know it, they are calling each other cunts and everything we work towards as Queens has been stripped back. So I remove the threads. It's always been less about protecting myself from everyone, and more about protecting everyone from everyone.

In Denim's case, 99% of the comments were kind. Some of my trolls piped in with: *He looks as feral as you Cunstance* and the occasional hater of Denim's would write something about his past.

Denim has a past. A fucking full-on one.

Death is the inevitable part of life. Sometimes it's fair and sometimes it's not. But it *always* hurts.

You will eventually get through losing a parent, you do eventually fix your own heart. They didn't give you life, only to take it away when they left. They gave you life to carry it on, long after they go. Your parents hurt when you hurt, so you fix yourself to honour their soul and carry on.

THE COLOURFUL, INTERESTING AND SOMETIMES FUCKED-UP HISTORY OF DENIM

If you ask Denim what the most important thing in his life is, he'd tell you his children. If you ask him what has shaped his life the most, he'd probably tell you drugs.

Denzy met Lisa through her older brother at nineteen; she was sixteen, and they fell in love. He lived in a beautiful country town on a stunning beach called Esperance; now it has a population of just under ten thousand, but when he was growing up it was a lot smaller.

Esperance has those beaches where the sand feels like flour on your feet and it actually squeaks, and even when the sky is overcast, the beach is always an illuminating turquoise.

Lisa was a young, beautiful blonde working in a surf shop and Denzy was a surfing, football-playing fella who by the time most of his mates had left school was a qualified carpenter. They kind of seemed perfect for each other, and she moved into his folks' place within just a few months of meeting one another.

They were inseparable, moving to Margaret River and living in a tent for a year, moving to Bussleton, going back to Esperance, buying a house and getting engaged before they knew it.

Sometimes I think it's the small country town, sometimes I think it's just addictive personalities, maybe sometimes it's just boredom. But to this day, Denim swears it wasn't to numb some kind of pain. For whatever reason, not long after Denim and Lisa together, they got heavily hooked on drugs. When they first met each other, she had only ever smoked joints, while he had only ever tried acid; but within a few short years, they would both be addicted to heroin.

Denzy doesn't speak badly of heroin. In fact, he speaks of it like she's an ex-lover who he shared some amazing times with, and some shitty ones. There are times where he misses it and times he says he is so grateful to be free of it. But he is never resentful of the years he lost.

He has told me a few times of how long it took him to actually enjoy heroin, or "Ham" as he calls it. He says that something about it makes you keep going back in the beginning, even though you're not really loving the dizzy, spewy feeling it gives you.

I have never tried heroin. I have had ecstasy that floored me and made my eyes roll to the back of my head, but never heroin. I suppose when your mum, stepdad, dad and other family members have all been addicted to it, the novelty is just never there. My mum and I have always been really open with each other about sex and drugs. She got clean; it was hard, but she raised me as a fine example of a sober mum and spoke to me about the struggles. That's all you can ask for as the daughter of a drug-addicted family – someone to lead by example, while warning you of the danger.

In the end, Denim told me that he thinks he was just as addicted to the needle as he was the drug. But soon began a long-term struggle between Lisa and Denim of trying to kick the habit, falling back into it and making huge life changes. Denim would dry out, a feeling he could only describe as feeling like death. He says he would sweat out a chemical smell and ache and sleep until he felt normal again, and usually do it all over again a few days later.

This was their life until they decided to make a geographical jump to get clean and get away from a life that wasn't working for them. They moved to Bunbury and Denim began a roof plumbing business; it was booming. Bunbury has a funny reputation. Just yesterday, I saw a viral video on Facebook of a street brawl that was filmed there. It's pretty, it has wild dolphins that swim to the shore for tourists to see, beautiful beaches… but it also has a drug problem.

Denim was making more money than he could dream of. They bought two houses, had a beautiful baby boy, Sunny, and got married.

Denim describes their marriage as usually happy; they had grown up together and were best friends. Lisa worried about everything and was easily agitated and they did have occasional huge fights, but she was a really good mum, organised and busy with Sunny. Times were good, and four years later, when business was still doing really well, they decided to have Zeyke.

Unfortunately, however, the drug habits returned with the money Denim's business brought in, and new connections in Bunbury. Denim remembers the exact night that they were at a party and someone there said they could score "Ham". And so began the worst of their addicted years. Everything fell apart.

Their habit was costing them over a thousand dollars a day and their youngest child was only one. Although in a similar situation to the one that I was brought up in, the children were still loved, clean, healthy and cared for perfectly. So many people are under the impression that if you are addicted to drugs, you must be a piece of shit parent, but I come from a family with a few functioning drug addicts, people who still put their children first, who never took them to dealers' houses or used drugs in front of them. I do believe that addiction is an illness, and child abuse is a crime, but they are two different things. Sunny and Zeyke were loved; they came first.

Lisa lost two of her brothers to drugs and Denim lost his best friend. Denim and his best friend had made each other necklaces to get clean, their theory being that when they were wearing them, they wouldn't touch drugs. In reality, the drugs were strong enough to make them take the necklaces off and get fucked up. Lisa and Denim both grieved hard but it wasn't enough to get them clean.

Denim told me that after her brothers died, he felt like he had lost Lisa, like he couldn't reach her anymore. She missed her brothers so much and was becoming a different person. She started to blame him for her not being able to get clean, and eventually she left him.

Denim tried everything to get Lisa back; she was his true love. When I first met him, I was jealous of the way that he spoke about her, he knew her inside and out. He lived his darkest moments after losing his marriage.

Lisa didn't know what she wanted. She still remained close to Denim and he would come and stay with them all when she would let him, and yet she was also seeing other people. They would fight, and he would have to leave again. Denim just wanted her back; he lived for the kids.

One day, she came over to pick up the kids. Denim got them in her car and she refused to unwind the window to talk to him. He was broken.

To be honest, I don't know exactly what happened in their marriage. Sometimes I ask questions, sometimes he tells me stories, sometimes neither of us want to know about our past relationships, and sometimes I feel like I am Lisa, and Denim pisses me off so much that I take her side in all the fights he tells me that they had.

So God knows why she didn't unwind her window to talk to him on this day, but she didn't. And to Denim, losing her and saying goodbye to his kids, losing everything he had ever known, the pain was unbearable. He called his dad, Ian, and told him he was going to end it all. By this time his parents were so accustomed to having a son who used drugs, that they knew what to do. "Don't hang up on me," Ian said.

And Denim just remembers hanging up.

And then shot up two grams of heroin.

Now, I don't know heroin talk, but I'm told that's enough to kill you twice. Thankfully, Ian called the drug counselling number. They sent the police to his house, who could see Denim lying on the kitchen floor through a window.

Denim recalls being in the ambulance; he said it felt like being in a tunnel where he could hear a lady's voice calling him. I thought he was talking about some existential angel, but he told me it was the ambulance officer. Apparently, he died three times on his way to hospital, where he was revived and forced to stay in psych overnight. To this day, he wishes could have thanked the paramedic who bought him back, but he never got the chance.

I asked him, "Were you trying to kill yourself?"

And he responded, "I don't know. I think I was just crying out for Lisa."

Lisa did show up at the hospital, told him he was an idiot and left.

If you judge someone on their past, you're going to miss all the colourful madness of the world.

THE MOTHER OF MY BEAUTIFUL STEPSONS

Denim has shared a lot of memories with me about his marriage and divorce from Lisa. He told me that she would call him when her new boyfriend wasn't around and confide in him, tell him she was wrong to think that his presence contributed to her own drug problems, and that she was just was bad alone. She would bitch about her new boyfriend, knowing all the while that with a click of her finger, she could have Denim back. He loved her unconditionally and, despite being the instigator of the divorce, it's obvious that she loved him too.

However, Denim never forgot the time she said, "I just want to be with my brothers."

Denim's life continued to spiral after the divorce. He stopped working, his drug use was at an all-time high, the darkest depression consumed him as he pined for his kids, until he finally hit the bottom, and made another call to his dad. "Dad, you have to come and get me."

Denim's dad came with a close family friend, Tom, who Denim calls his "beach dad", because he taught him how to surf and they spent many nights together camping on the beach.

Denim told me that his dad walked into his house, saw the state of the place he had been living in, saw the state of his son, and walked out visibly devastated. Tom followed him out, put his arm around him and said, "It will be OK. We will clean the place up, one thing at a time."

And together they sorted out the house and mess that Denim was calling home.

They brought Denim back to Esperance, to their farm, and to what Denim refers to as his "farm rehab". His mum and dad cleaned him up. It didn't happen overnight. It took a lot longer than that. And Denim is very well aware that not everyone is as lucky as he is, to have parents so prepared to drop everything and put 100% into getting a grown man on his feet, a man who had every opportunity to help himself and never managed to. He is eternally grateful for that, and I think in some ways, it has shown him how to be the dad that he is today.

During this time, he was a part-time dad. He saw the kids during the school holidays. They would meet halfway between both their towns, about two and a half hours' drive each. Denim would stay at his grandma's house the night before the pick-up, as it was close to the meeting point. His mum told me that he would sleep on the floor in the lounge room, because it was closest to the door, so that in the morning he could jump up and fly out the door.

They were all he looked forward to, all he lived for. His parents would take time off and they'd all take the boys camping and fishing. To this day, they are filled with nothing but fun memories with their dad.

Obviously I have never met Lisa. I believe I live with the man that knew her best and her two beautiful boys. Her mental health is rarely spoken about; in fact, Denim and the boys had a pact that they would only ever speak about her in light and in love.

I have met her best friends and her sister-in-law but never her parents. We were trolled for a while by someone close to Lisa, telling Denim that he is writing too much about my kids and not enough about his, asking him if he is "pussy whipped" and similar rantings. I can only put it down to hurt; they have lost a lot and have decided to turn some hate our way.

Someone close to Lisa told me that she was diagnosed with bipolar before she died. Denim doesn't know much about her life just before she died as she had a new partner, and while they still had their chats and handovers with the children, all he knew was that she was still into drugs – different ones, like methamphetamines.

This same friend told me that Lisa wanted to commit suicide but had spoken about wanting to do it in a way that the boys wouldn't find her. I wasn't there, and neither was Denim. We don't know what her support network was like at the time. He doesn't know the details. He received a phone call one morning while he was in Perth from her partner of the time, asking him if he had seen Lisa; he hadn't. From Denim's understanding, she and her partner had had an argument and Lisa stormed out. The following morning she was still missing, and that's when he called Denim. Denim then called him back later that afternoon, worried about Lisa. And then his phone call was returned within half an hour; Lisa had hung herself in the backyard of an empty house down the road.

Denim sped straight to his sons. He told Lisa's partner, who he did not get on with at all, to dare not tell the boys until he got there. Denim was with Lisa for thirteen years, and still to that day, he loved her. Dealing with his own shock and trying to be the father these poor boys needed is the hardest thing I have ever had to hear coming out of the mouth of the man I love.

He arrived and took them for the weekend, away from the grief and uncertainty at their home. They played in the sunshine while Denim got his head around breaking it to his little boys that their mum wasn't coming back. There is no right way to say it, no rulebook, nobody you can call.

At the end of the weekend he took them home and sat them down, and he told them that Mum had hurt herself, very badly and she wasn't coming back. And after a few moments they all took it in and understood what it meant.

Sunny was eleven and Zeyke only seven.

And how they handled it, how they grieved, is their story to tell, not Denim's and certainly not mine.

Denim visited the house that Lisa died in. He doesn't understand how she did it, he was kept in the dark as all ex-partners are when there is a death; it's like your history dies with them and no matter how little time is spent with new partner, it all becomes about them. What happened that night, the argument, a smashed computer, it will all remain a mystery, only understood by those who won't or can't share the truth.

When I first met Denim, he told me that his ex-wife was the kind of woman who would jump out of a moving car if you pissed her off, and continue to storm off. He said that he would follow her until she came back in, fiery and beautiful. He would wait however long she needed. He believed he should have followed her; he believes she would still be here if they hadn't broken up.

Within two weeks Denim had organised permanent accommodation so the kids could live with him. And aside from some time that Sunny spent with his grandparents, so began the journey of the three of them – healing, loving and adventures. Now sixteen, Sunny is the most responsible kid you'll ever meet. He came out of the womb a joy, barely cried, smiled all day, loved his breastmilk and made them nothing but happy. And to this day, he reflects that baby, only now he is also clever and kind and the perfect big brother. Our family joke is "ask Sunny" because Denzy and I are as useless as each other, the rest of the kids are busy fighting or whinging, and Sunny knows *everything*. He directs us, knows what gates to go to at the airport and just generally keeps everyone's shit together.

Zeyke is the opposite: a typical youngest child, full of adventure and no consequences, cheeky and sweet. Kind and helpful but always up to something. Zeyke went with Denim straight away, no need for structure and never questioning where they would live or what they would do, happy for adventure.

Denim went back to work. He provided for the kids, tried to start a life for them all but it just didn't feel right – the kids needed more. They needed to heal, and a structured life didn't feel right after everything they had been through.

That's when Denim made the decision he was dropping out of the system, of the wheel of life, of the expectations. He threw away all of his possessions and dragged Sunny and Zeyke out of school, bought a bus and embarked on a trip around the whole country. After the year the kids had been through, he just wanted to give them freedom – freedom to feel and heal and be themselves. Being a surfer, he assumed when he asked them what they wanted to do around the country, they would say, "Surf every break we can find," but instead they both said,

"Skate every skate park we find," and so that's exactly what they did.

They fought in the bus, played music, slept wherever they could park it, snuck into all-ages music festivals, scraped together what money they could for food, slept in a graveyard, met homeless people, travellers, families, and kept moving, kept going and healed.

Sunny told me that their trip is what made the boys the skaters they are today, to be able to skate at so many different parks. Now when there is a competition on, they can find their way around any foreign skate park extremely quickly.

I don't think you ever really heal from losing your mum. I don't think that chapter will ever be closed. I know that they miss her. When they talk about her, it's always funny stories, and respect and love just oozes out of them as they remember the beautiful woman she was. They were just boys of seven and eleven years old when she left.

But all you need to do is ask them and they will tell you that Dad stepped up in the most unconventional way. "Dad is a legend."

Denim was never entirely clean until he had his kids full-time. He now lives and breathes for his boys. He can't pinpoint the day that it happened or an event that changed him, but he knows it was the boys – the love he has for them saved him, so that he could save them.

When I first met him, I was perplexed by so many things – how little regard he had for society's expectations, how polite and respectful his children were, and no matter what the kids were asking for, he'd do. Living on the single parent's pension in a shared house, they didn't have much but whatever they had went on the boys. They always had friends sleeping over, if they wanted to go skating in the middle of the night to a park an hour's drive away, he just didn't mind.

It just all seemed so free.

Create a world where mental illness and physical illness are treated equally. Suicide is a terminal result to a misunderstood chronic illness.

WHERE IT ALL BEGINS: ONLINE BULLYING

So back to online bullying. You hear the words, you scroll past the stories; it doesn't really affect you, does it?

I mean, you're not being bullied. If you were, you'd delete the cunts and move on. But what about our kids? I honestly don't know how I have been lucky enough to reach the level of success that I have achieved. You become immune to it, so when other people see you as this extremely successful person, it is very confusing because it is in no way how you see yourself.

A couple of weeks ago, I wrote a blog that reached 32 million people. Did my life change? Not one bit, it's so easy to not see it.

When I first started blogging, I was the underdog, and everyone loves the underdog. I was everyone's secret little indulgence, they indulged in listening to me bitch about my life and they loved it. I was the funny little bogan from Perth who loved to bitch about relationships and her kids, her bankcard declining, and flick the bird to the world.

I was cheered on by every other chick who woke up in the morning thinking, "Fuck this for a cruel joke! Why the fuck is my husband doing 40-hour weeks while I do 168-hour weeks and still get accused of "not working"; and by all of those chicks who woke up with the accusation of "not coping", because her stretched out tits, tummy and fanny don't give her that after-birth "glow" that the magazines told her she should be rocking.

I was a nobody, and I was reminding us all that we were somebody.

Everyone wants to be different in a cool way; they want to like the bands that nobody else likes, they don't want to follow the herd – nobody wants to be mainstream. I'm no different; following the herd is my idea of hell. I don't listen to mainstream or pop music. I'd like to say that I don't shop at Cotton On, but fuck it, of course I do.

So, the more people started to like me, the more people turned, and... I became mainstream. When you have over a million followers, it becomes "different" to not like me, and all of a sudden, people were feeling validated for hating me. It made them feel different: "How cool am I for hating this thing that everyone loves..."

I don't do anything to incite this hatred. I once had a PR chick tell me that she studied what happened to me, and how quickly I went from being Australia's most loved to Australia's most hated, and she concluded that I did nothing. I didn't change at all. It was always going to happen; successful women aren't tolerated, much less the successful underdogs. The general public love an underdog, as long as she knows her place and never steps over the line. They like Aboriginals until they start to claim rights; they love homosexuals until one is making out in public. They tolerate transgender kids, but when they start asking for unisex toilets in schools, they're "expecting special treatment". They liked Rosie Batty; how could they not? She was thrown into the public eye when her abusive ex murdered her son, and she took her grief and started a foundation. She has worked tirelessly for sufferers of domestic violence and was awarded "Australian of the Year", but many people turned when she started earning a wage and accepting the worth of her public speaking.

The minute the underdog realises her own worth, she has become too big for her boots. The message is: be the underdog, but never own any success that comes from your struggles. And as much as I was advised of this, my success was staring everyone in the eye with the numbers that followed my posts and with the number of followers I had on my page.

And so the comments began:

I used to like her until she…

She's a shit mum who exploits her children.

She stinks.

And then the hate groups formed.

The first one was called something like "The Purge". It had my picture and was filled with comments about how fucked up I am, what kind of violent acts people wanted to perform on me, fabrications of what must go on at my house with my children. My every word taken out of context, my "fat" stomach ripped apart.

I reported it to Facebook once with no response but the second time I reported it, Facebook found it to be a hate group and pulled it down. Only the creators of the group were having too much fun, so they started another one called "The Abdication of Constance Hall". Then they got a bit smarter; well, as smart as internet trolls can be, and they crossed less technical boundaries. My private Facebook page was hacked, people created fake profiles of friends of mine and friend requested me then screenshot posts about my mum, my kids, everything. The things that happened in this group tore me apart.

I'm not squeaky-clean; I'm far from it and I've never pretended otherwise. My Facebook is filled with horrible jokes from over the years. My brother and I have been hacking into each other's Facebook for years, accusing each other of itchy dicks and crushes on exes.

My brother and I have a terrible personal joke that Santa Claus is a paedophile. Crass, I know; in fact, all of my siblings and cousins have way too many pedo jokes. Uncles don't get through Christmas dinners without pedo accusations; all in humour, dark humour, a humour that knows no boundaries.

So when my mum sent me a picture of my kids on Santa Claus' knee, kind of to tease me because she knows that I'd never do the department store "Santa pic" thing as it just reminds me of the greed that is Christmas, my brother got hold of my phone and uploaded the picture with the caption: *Thanks Mum for finding a fat pedo and lending him my kids for an hour.*

I should have taken it down, but before I was famous I didn't really think much of Facebook. It was just for friends and family, and obviously my family would see the humour, poor taste family joke and all, and I completely forgot about it. Until years later, when I had a hate group and they broke into my private Facebook account. They trolled through years of my private postings, found that post, screenshot it and sent it to every media outlet in Australia, put it in every group, including Kmart Mums and, of course, my hate groups.

I was sent message after message, asking me to explain myself. Not knowing what to do, I called my PR and said, "Umm… I kind of fucked up again."

She said, "Surely it's photoshopped, it couldn't have come from your Facebook?"

And I was all, "Fuck, man, I never claimed to be politically correct… or a decent human… "

Together, we decided to say nothing. Blaming my brother would throw him under the bus, even though when I told him, he pissed himself laughing and told me he couldn't give a fuck. Lying by saying it was photoshopped would actually feel wrong and give me major anxiety about getting caught.

It still pops up all the time, in the comment sections of media stories about me. The trolls have given it a huge backstory, saying that I posted it publicly to crucify the Santa Claus actor because he pissed me off, saying that he lost his job because of the photo, saying that he killed himself because of it all. I just have to read on as if I'm reading about someone else's life, because it's that fucking absurd.

I've had photos of myself crying turned into memes. I've even had the memes printed out on paper and put up throughout Perth. I've had exes sent naked selfies of my trolls' bodies. I've had my ABN number published with a post egging each other on to call the tax department because I wasn't registered for GST (I trade under a company name and wouldn't be dumb enough to not pay GST in my position.)

My partner, his children, my children, have all been attacked. I've been pulled out of public events due to threats of violence, told to kill myself and, probably most hurtfully, I have found that old friends of mine were under fake names in my hate group, giving away private information, including my phone number.

I've been turned on by people I considered friends, all so that they could get their five minutes. It's insane. My open life that I'd share with anyone has had its hatches battened down to the point that my circle of trust went from being millions of people to being a handful.

But why?

What doesn't kill you makes you stronger... and stronger until you're the fiercest Xena bitch that you can be, ready to take on *all* the cunts.

CYBERBULLIES, TROLLS AND KEYBOARD WARRIORS

Why do people feel the need to online bully? Trolling tends to happen to people like me a lot; any story you read about a woman with a high profile, or anyone in the public eye, will get trolled. Trolling is kind of not even personal for the troll – it's a game they like to play, a game with no winners or losers, only victims and perpetrators.

Trolls

Trolling is attention-seeking from a hidden account or from a fake name. A troll is desperate to get some eyes on him or her for a reaction, but not the real them. Fuck no, stay the fuck away from the real troll, because they believe themselves as unworthy as they come.

A troll drags the attention away from the story or author and makes it about themselves, with a comment that will shock readers out of the topic of conversation and into their world.

For example, I will be trolled after a story about my children hits the news and a troll will disregard the content of the story and write a highly educated comment like: *Constance Hall is a fat slut*.

Instead of commenting on the story, a commenter will then feel obliged to respond to the troll, telling them what a holy fuckbrain they are, and the troll wins; they got the attention they were seeking.

Just like my twins. Rumi, who's three, will scream at me for a Le Snack (I'm a Le Snack Nazi because I only ever buy enough for lunches, and if I have to go to Woolworths one more time than I planned to in a week, someone's gonna pay). If I give it to him, he will keep screaming for something else. He is basically just screaming for my attention.

He's the kitchen version of a troll. Hear that mums? Our kids are trolling us in the kitchen. A troll doesn't care. A troll lacks empathy and couldn't give a shit if their victim is suicidal or partying as long as they receive the desired attention.

Does it hurt? No. Trolls are pathetic, like three-year-olds wanting Mama to look at them instead of the stove or computer or her Tinder account, and their words are too stupid to dig deep.

I remember the exact words written about me on the bus stop outside our school. I went to catch the bus home after school and the words *Constance Hall is a fucking fat slut* were written in black permanent marker on it. Was I hurt? Yes, I was devastated. That was bullying. They knew me, and they knew all of my friends would see it. I pretended not to be hurt, laughed it off. Went home and cried my eyes out. (I later learnt that there is nothing wrong with being a fat slut. You meet a guy, you both like each other, you get fingered, eaten out, fucked properly and if he knows what's good for him you both get to share Maccas for brekkie. Fuckers need a new insult, coz that's living the dream in my eyes.)

Cyberbullies

Cyberbullies are a different kettle of fish. A cyberbully is less about gaining attention for themselves and more about hurting people. Cyberbullying has been linked to narcissism and psychopathy.

A cyberbully will share intimate photos, memes, harass inboxes, set up hate groups with the goal of hurting, humiliating and destroying their victims. A cyberbully will suffer if their victim is not suffering. A cyberbully will fail if their victim is not hurt or humiliated.

Keyboard Warriors

So what about the keyboard warrior? Well, that, is simply a cross between them both: they exhibit the attention-seeking traits of a troll, with the desire to pull down and cause hurt to the victim. A keyboard warrior causes more danger to the internet on a broader perspective, because their passive-aggressive nature makes their comments pass as rational. A sheep in wolf's clothing or, you might say, a troll in warrior armour.

At the end of the day a keyboard warrior, like a troll and a cyberbully, has bad intentions; and, to be frank, the only quality I give a fuck about in someone is their intentions.

And so the saying goes: "Don't feed the trolls". It's valid advice; if they are not getting the attention that they want, then they will go away. Just like my little Rumi, hassling the shit out of me in the kitchen. If I ignore him and stop giving into his ridiculous three-year-old demands, he'll get bored and go troll his sister.

But how the fuck are we going to combat cyberbullies?

Firstly, I'd like to ask the question: Why? Why do we need to combat them? If they really are narcissists, why do we even care about them?

Because, unlike school, we can't just dob on them and be done with it. There is nobody to dob to. There are no teachers and no police. When we were bullied at school, we were bullied at school and at the bus stop, and while the feelings came home with us, the bullying didn't and we were safe eating dinner with our mums and safe in our beds.

But cyberbullying is today's real-life horror film. It is relentless and it never stops.

I have lived it. I am a 34-year-old woman, who earns a good living, has family, friends and employees who all support me, and I have lived the horror film. If I am completely honest, it has made me consider driving myself into a tree at times. If I didn't have my children, I probably would have.

Trolls. Fake accounts, stupid cartoon profile pictures and dumb names. Attention is the main game. The person they are trolling usually displays qualities that make trolls feel inadequate. Report them but ignore them. Never, ever bother engaging with someone who doesn't even have the guts to show their identity. Trolls only win when you engage with them.

Cyberbullying is different. They are relentlessly trying to hurt someone. Cyberbullying has been linked to narcissism and psychopathy. They are dangerous and must be reported/acted on. Do not "fight back" online. Report to authorities, schools, children's parents, employers, etc.

Keyboard warriors have bad intentions. Causing friction online and bringing people down because they aren't feeling too good about themselves. An old quote that I've heard a few times now and definitely relates to this area: "Be careful when fighting with pigs. You'll both end up covered in shit but the pig will enjoy it."

TODAY, YOUR KIDS' BULLIES ARE HAVING DINNER WITH THEM, ON THE TOILET WITH THEM AND THE LAST PEOPLE TO SPEAK TO THEM AT NIGHT

So how do we protect our children from being bullied online? Isn't that kind of like saying, "How do we teach our daughters to not get raped?"

Have you ever heard that saying, if you give them enough rope, they will hang themselves? That's what the internet has become to our children, teenagers in particular. A whole lot of rope – and they are hanging themselves.

It's almost unfair. Most teenagers don't yet have the emotional intelligence to understand what they are doing. Even my best friend told me that she is only now realising that she was a bully in high school, teasing the younger children or the ones with fewer friends. At the time, she knew she was wasn't being nice, but she had no idea that she could have been hurting someone to the point of causing depression or considering taking their own lives.

With social media, it's even easier to be relentless, to make each other feel alone, trapped, humiliated. It's almost like handing a three-year-old a loaded gun and expecting nobody to get hurt.

I wish I could just pull my kids out. If there was an opt-out button for the internet and social media I'd press it. If there was an opt-out button for mothering them during their teenage years, I'd press it. If there was an opt-out button for adulting in general, I'd have fucking pressed it. But alas, we push through.

How do we teach our children to be respectful and unaffected by disrespectful behaviour on the internet when we still don't know?

The first step is to check our own behaviour.

I always remember a conversation I had with my psychologist a few years ago on my social media behaviour. She asked me to recognise what my heart rate and stress levels were doing while I was online. I was pregnant at the time (the internet is riddled with furious pregnant chicks. Nobody loves a war of the words like a pregnant chick; we are offended by everything. If I saw a post on breastfeeding, it offended me for non-breastfeeders, and if I saw a post on bottle milk, I'd slam it with some "breast is best" facts). The internet was my boxing ring, and the worst part? I'd get highly offended when anyone fought back. I defined keyboard warrior, and it was a direct reflection of my state of mind. I was depressed, so I wasn't happy unless my life reflected that depression. I was inviting in drama so that I didn't have to confront my depression. It validated my unhappiness.

This realisation was everything. My heart was racing all the time. I'd get on the internet, have a virtual punch-up and get off feeling hugely anxious. And none of it was worth it; it could have all been avoided. So my homework was to get off the internet.

My psych wanted me switch off for a week and instead only have face-to-face contact for that whole week. Every day, I had to meet a friend out of the house for a coffee and a chat and, if

I was feeling extra generous to my mental state of mind, go for a walk as well.

Never having been good with homework, I wasn't exactly going to stick to it. I compromised with myself, had only face-to-face contact and I got out of the house and went for a walk.

I found it all hugely beneficial to my wellbeing and depression, but I figured she probably didn't realise that as a housewife who doesn't clean, I'd literally have nothing to do if I shunned social media.

So I fast-tracked my homework, realising she didn't want me off the internet, but rather she wanted me to only use it to make myself feel good, which meant I had to stop keyboard warrior-ing.

So I became mature and scrolled past things that offended me. I did not engage unless it was to show support. It was the most freeing thing for my mental state and I got to keep my Facebook. Win-win!

Denim has a lovely, cruisy, surfer friend with long blond hair, who never bitches about anyone. Denim told me that if you say anything bad about anyone to him, he responds, "He's just doing his thing, man". As in, that's their journey and you know nothing about it. Why bitch? Which can be really frustrating when you just want to have a bloody bitch! But seriously, it's true – we all know that.

And so it became the new mantra inside my head. When I see folks I don't agree with preaching all over the internet, I tell myself, "They're just doing their thing, man" and I scroll on.

I encourage anyone who's wanting to show their kids how to use the internet safely, or who is just wanting to make it a happier place, to be aware of your own internet habits. Find out what's pissing you off and why and don't forget that whatever anyone else is doing, "they're just doing their thing, man."

But for something as serious as this is, something that's killing children in communities all over the world, I wanted to get some advice from an expert.

ONLINE BULLYING - BY MICHAEL CARR-GREGG AND SUSAN MCLEAN

It was her face that caught our attention. Dolly, aka Amy Jayne Everett, who at the age of six was the face of the iconic hat brand, Akubra, beaming out her trillion-kilowatt smile. Incredibly, she is now dead – having taken her own life at the age of fourteen after being cyber-bullied.

Her death generated horror and sadness in homes around Australia, and the nation seemed to pause for a moment to grieve. Then the grief gave way to anger and frustration at our helplessness in the face of this tragedy. Even the PM posted on Facebook, saying his heart was breaking for Dolly and her family: "Dolly's passing highlights the devastating impact that bullying can have on its victims… every step must be taken to reduce the incidence of bullying, whether offline or on, and eliminate it wherever we can."

So can we ever entirely eliminate online bullying? As two of Australia's leading cyber-safety educators who have been dealing with the fallout of cyberbullying for decades, we fear that the answer is no, but we both believe that there is more Australia can do to address the issue.

So why is vanquishing all cyberbullying so hard?

1) Bill Belsey's "perfect storm"

Bill was the first person to use the term "cyberbully", and he speaks of the "perfect storm" of the immature teenage brain combining with a technology that is of the moment and in the moment.

Bill is referring to the fact that the human brain has 100 billion brain cells, 1000 trillion connections, and they are not wired up yet. More importantly, between the age of twelve and young adulthood, there's a loss of this grey matter. It's losing perhaps 30,000 connections per second in a frenzy of brain remodelling. The last part of the brain to develop is the prefrontal lobe – in charge of planning, and impulse control.

Essentially the brain brakes aren't yet developed, but the accelerator is flat to the floor – by puberty. Add to this a special vulnerability to peer pressure, a desire to be accepted, a lack of emotional empathy and the potential for cyberbullying is clearly present. It unsurprisingly peaks around transition to high school.

2) Lack of parental supervision

It has been often said that there is no such thing as a perfect parent – and the number of adult carers who allow their children under the age of thirteen on social media is growing. This is problematic as young children, for the reasons mentioned in point 1 often do not have the emotional, psychological or social maturity to manage a digital footprint or think before they click. In this age of laissez-faire parenting, too many parents seem to have thrown in the digital towel, caved to pester power and are buying smart phones for their under thirteen-year-olds. You can still have security and text messages with a dumb phone. The excuse of, "I don't get it," or "I don't use tech" are well past their use by date. Being an effective parent in the 21st century means you must be able to actively parent in the digital space. Educate yourself now!

3) Lack of cyber safety education

In the UK, cyber safety education in primary schools is mandatory, and schools are graded on it when the OFSTED inspector pays a visit, yet in Australia this is not the case. We have available to all schools the eSmart school framework, which was developed by RMIT University in consultation with cyber safety, bullying, education and industry experts from across Australia.

In 2010, eSmart was piloted in 159 schools across Australia with funding from the Commonwealth Department of Education. In some states like Victoria, the state government has made eSmart Schools available to every government school and 300 Catholic and independent schools at no charge. In addition, each of these schools received a $2,000 grant to assist in the implementation of the framework. An initiative of The Alannah and Madeline Foundation, the framework helps support schools to embrace the benefits of technology and ensure they are doing everything possible to reduce students' exposure to cyber-risks. It targets teachers, students and parents and it identifies what the school is doing well, and where it's failing. It then comes up with an individual solution for individual schools. It allows all schools to find their individual and unique route to the same final destination. No other plan does any of that. We both believe that if we are to honour the legacy of Dolly and others who have taken their life, then eSmart must become mandatory in every primary school across Australia. And then with further funding, be mandated in secondary schools. Perhaps the PM needs to intervene here.

4) The social media companies

While some are doing an outstanding job of promoting the wellbeing of its users, others are not.

A few weeks ago, a "cewebwerty" on YouTube called Logan Paul, with no less than six million followers, took a camera crew into a primeval forest at the foot of Mount Fuji called Aokigahara. The forest is a known suicide hot spot and his crew stumbled upon someone who had taken their own life. They then proceeded to post a video of the body hanging from a tree for his tweenage fans. The clip was eventually taken down, but YouTube were mute for ten days before issuing an apology.

In January last year a twelve-year-old girl, Katelyn Nicole Davis, livestreamed her own death by hanging, after alleging she was abused by a relative. The video went viral and was replayed on many websites. We must keep the pressure on these companies to ensure that safety is a key component of their business plan, rather than an add-on after a tragedy. We must also actively promote those taking these issues seriously and name those who don't!

5) Anonymity

In the olden days, bullies were more easily identified. Consequences ranged from being suspended from school, to being banned from activities and venues, to even being arrested. But cyberbullies are more elusive. The perceived anonymity of the internet allows for the type of disinhibition, a kind of digital Dutch courage, that makes cyberbullies, especially children, bolder in their attacks. We must ensure that law enforcement have the knowledge and training to be able to provide an acceptable level of response in the investigation of all forms of online abuse, especially in the tracing of the so called "anonymous" accounts.

Albert Camus said, "suicide, like a great work of art, is prepared within the silence of the heart" and indeed the reality is that no one will ever know precisely the nature and extent of Dolly's psychological demons. Nor will we know if she was suffering from a mental illness and the cyberbullying simply exacerbated it and acted as a trigger. But if we are to accede to Dolly's family's wishes, the social media companies, parents, schools and the Federal and State governments can and should do more.

*

I'm far from healed from the pain that the online bullies caused me. There are still days that I don't want to get out of bed, entire days my moderators have to spend taking off all the nasty comments, so I can't post at all.

But I realised that I was given haters as a gift. I turned my loneliness into a blog, and my struggles with parenting into a book, and the fact that I looked like a boiled egg in all the clothes I wore into a clothing line. My haters came to me so that I would stop dismissing online bullying, so that I could use my platform as a place that refuses to be a part of the problem, so that I can talk to and listen to young people instead of issuing a patronising "just switch off". I can recognise the pain and the fear of not knowing what will be said next. Together, with over a million Queens, I think we can make a real difference.

Lead by example. What are you doing online? Some "mother's groups" online are full of abuse and bullying and teasing and ganging up. If you are part of one, leave it.

"They are just doing their thing babe." Don't let it upset you. She might be having a bad day, or a great day. It's not your day. Just keep scrolling, turn the internet around – ignore the bad and praise the good.

TRYING TO CONVINCE DENIM I'M A SULTRY SEX SYMBOL

HE PULLED A BUG
OUT OF MY HAIR!

The evening after I posted the blog about Denim, I went to the skate park. Denim hadn't been online all day, and I knew that when he didn't have money for phone credit to use the internet he was reliant on a particular spot in his backyard where he could tune in to the wi-fi from the backpacker's next-door. As I didn't have his mobile number, only his Facebook, I didn't even know if he had seen the post.

Eventually, he turned it on, saw a message from me saying: *Skate Park?*

And told me he'd be there in five. He rocked up with a six-pack of Coronas; I had a six-pack of Coronas too.

Denim was wearing a blue flannelette top and shorts; I was wearing one of my Mumtum skirts and a huge jumper (uniform).

We talked about the post while the kids skated. He was a little overwhelmed and a little shocked but was determined to respond to everyone's comments individually, which I thought was equally admirable and cute, considering there were around 4,000 of them.

We sat around for ages, talking and laughing; not just us, there were other mums there too. Everything was really casual and normal, just a bunch of mates, which felt lovely in a new town. Until something happened, something that nobody else will care about or see the significance of, but I did.

A bug flew into my hair.

I didn't notice it. I was sitting on the floor; I'm a floor sitter, always have been and I'm at my most comfortable at someone's house if sitting on their floor. Denim was sitting on the bench and saw the bug fly into my hair. He got up immediately, came over to me and pulled the bug out of my hair.

Shocked, I asked, "What are you doing?"

He responded, "Something flew into your hair. I got it."

A girlfriend and I shot each other a quick glance. You have to know me personally to understand why this is so weird, why this isn't just a friendly man helping out his mate. People don't touch me, especially not men. It all changed with the fame. People are intimidated by me; me, the least intimidating person on earth. When women get to know me, and realise how much of a touching creep I am, they let down their barriers and become touchy too, but I couldn't tell you the last time a man had touched me. They are all either too petrified or just don't care.

No man I knew would have done that and I don't know if the realisation that a simple bug being pulled out of my hair was ground-breaking, excited me or depressed me.

Had I become so desperate that this was all it took to blow my mind? Like that dickhead guy who goes to the bar and the bartender gives him the minimal attention her job requires, and he returns to his table with the statement, "She wants me". No. She doesn't want him.

Was I really the female equivalent? "He pulled a bug out of my hair, OMG, OMG, he loves me."

The conversation moved to my kids. "You haven't met my

twins yet have you, Denim? If you had, you probably wouldn't be here."

I don't bring them to the skate park. One of the benefits of living with my nannies is that I don't have to run around skate parks like a headless chook, with the twins running every different direction possible.

"Nope I haven't," Denim responded, "but maybe I love kids and this is exactly where I would be."

I may have orgasmed at that point, or an ovary punched me in the tummy, screaming, "Give Me Dick!" Isn't that something that men say in movies and dreams? It's not something they say in real life, it's not something sexy surfer–skater dads say to mothers with four kids.

It came time to call it a night. The kids were getting tired, mum of the year had got them fish and chips for dinner, enough for all the kids at the skate park. I'm a sucker for communal eating.

I decided to leave my car at the skate park. I'd drunk most of my six-pack, bar a couple I gave away. Plus, the kids love walking home.

Denim was still under the limit and he told me he'd prefer it if he could drive our car home, informing me that our neighbourhood isn't as safe as I assumed. He only lives around the corner from me and could walk home from there; both of his kids had already walked home.

Accepting that lift was compromising, I knew it. But at that moment, I didn't care.

Denim put Arlo on his shoulders and Billie-Violet begged for her turn, and we walked to my car. After I put the kids to bed, Denim and I learnt for the first time that we could talk forever, about everything. We spoke about past relationships, music, art, celebrities, politicians. We drank beer and chatted on my daybed until midnight.

It was dark outside, we could barely see each other. At one point, he asked me if we could swap places because the light was shining on him and he wanted to be able to see me. I obliged, unsure of what was going on. Most of the signs pointed towards the beginning of a beautiful friendship. I just wasn't used to a man who actually just wanted the company of a woman, one on one. I was confused, closed to the idea of new love, yet this incredible man sat in front of me showing all the signs to not wanting love, just friendship… and I couldn't think of anything but love.

I have always landed straight into another man's arms. It seemed to be a pattern in my life, you know, to help you get over one man, you get straight under another one? It always ended in tears and there was always a price to pay. And fuck, did I pay in so many ways.

Someone once told me that when things have ended badly, they haven't really ended at all. When you jump into a new relationship to heal the pain of the last one, and the time comes to really sort out the issues of the last one, you realise that you've gone and fucked it.

I have learnt and paid so much, I wasn't going to go down the same path and repeat past mistakes. I needed space before I even looked at getting my freak on again.

The beers gave me confidence and made me a little curious, wondering what this guy wanted, what was he doing here, and I decided to put my foot on him, a trick I learnt in high school – if you've been friend-zoned, he will pat it; if you're lover-zoned, he will rub it.

For some reason at 33, with a 42-year-old man on my day bed, I thought that the same rules would apply. Alas, he didn't fall into the trap, no patting of the foot, and definitely no rubbing. He did however grab it, between his thumb and his finger.

What the fuck was that supposed to mean? Kind of like the way you would squeeze your kid's foot if it landed on your lap. "He must think I'm such a fuckhead, if I yank it away now I'm an even bigger creep." Argh, I was doing my own head in.

I'm not a patient woman. When I fall, I fall hard and when I'm over it, I leave fast. I don't give things time to grow because I do my own head in and with four children, I don't have time to do my own head in.

I grew bored. Denim picked up on it and said, "Shall we have another beer or are you done?"

I said, "I'm done, going to bed."

He got up and wrapped his arms around me, giving me a massive friend-zone hug. To make sure, because I am that desperate loser that needs to prove that a guy doesn't love me, I pulled my head out of the hug and smiled at him, the perfect time to kiss me if he was that way inclined. He was not.

So it was a fleeting moment of flirtation with no harm done. My heart skipped a few beats that night, but only to remind me that it still existed. I walked upstairs to my bed, where the only arms that I have slept inside and woken up inside in years, were waiting for me: Arlo's. And that was good enough for me.

That night, some paranoia slipped in. I messaged Denim asking him to be really careful not to talk about anything that we spoke about, to anyone, because I live in a different world to everyone else. I have an arch-nemesis waiting for me to fall, investigating my life constantly, laughing at me, bribing my friends, and that nemesis is called the media and it leaves me anxious and paranoid at every turn.

Scrolling through my Facebook feed and seeing my face on a news article sends a chill down my spine. You never know what it is that they are pulling up now, what words are being taken out of context, what angle they will take for the feeding frenzy of hate to get off on.

I just thank my lucky stars that I never made a sex tape, but even that thought sends a chill. I mean, there were some pretty sketchy nights out in my youth...

Denim responded with: *Anything that is ever said between you and I will always remain between you and I. I'll delete our messages. I got you, girl.*

Asking myself to stop reading into his kind nature as some sort of sign of his love for me, and then ignoring myself and grinning, I fell asleep.

There had been a void for so long; not just in the form of a lover, but I had also stopped having male friends. The men I was friends with kept a firm but respectful distance, so having Denim around was different and fun.

He started teaching my kids how to skate; his kids are first and second in the state for skateboarding and they owe a lot of that to Denim's training. Of course they have worked their little arses off at the skate parks, pushing themselves, exhausting themselves, but Denim was always by their side, showing them their limits. At the drop of a hat, he'd drive hours to a new skate park just to see them happy. My kids grew confident and we all seemed happy, in a non-romantic way.

Until one night.

Redefine romance. What is it to you? Surely you're as sick of flowers as I am.

Flirt. Kiss. Drink beer and make the first move, they can only say no.

FAIL

I was at home, bored and a bit drunk, a terrible combination for me. Bored is fine, drunk is fine, but both will lead to embarrassment.

I had put all the kids to sleep and done everything I needed to do to call myself a responsible mum. Why my phone doesn't come with a breathalyser is beyond me – I shouldn't be trusted. I made up the excuse that I needed to get money out of the ATM for my kids' school lunches in the morning and I had to walk to get it. I subtly messaged Denim that I was walking up, he could meet me at the end of his road, which was on the way, and reminded him that if he refused I could be raped and murdered. Yep, I'm cringing too…

Denim reluctantly agreed to come, too respectful to remind me that nothing was stopping me from getting cash out for their lunches in the morning or, you know, driving.

I walked up my hill and he was waiting for me on the corner of my street, looking handsome in baggy jeans, a black jumper and a beanie. I was wearing a slouchy Spell jumper (my favourite jumper as it makes me look effortlessly cool) a long skirt that I tie up with a big knot, and my hair was in a messy bun.

I thought I looked banging. Denim didn't mention anything. So we walked and talked and laughed, like we so easily do. I learnt a lot about Denim that night, a lot about his past and who he was. I touched his hair for the first time and realised it was dreadlocked like mine. He was barefoot despite the fact that it was a freezing cold night.

As we were walking up the hill after he met me, Denim told me that he'd been sick. He just sort of blurted it out: "You know I have Hepatitis C"? He said it casually, but I kind of felt like his casual way was a defence mechanism in anticipation of judgement.

I responded with, "My…" and I hesitated. I was about to say my dad died of hepatitis, until I realised how insensitive that would come across. In fact, some members of my family have, or have had, hepatitis. It has run rampant through all the people I know who were once addicted to heroin, and I knew that Denim was once an addict.

I am comfortable around Hep C. I know how you catch it and most importantly, I know how you don't. A lot of people are confused as to how you can catch it. People think it's like HIV and STDs, but it's spread through the blood and I'm not about to have anal tearing, foreskin tearing, wild sex, so I don't fear it. I accept it. Like I have ulcerative colitis and autoimmune inflammation of the bowel disease, Denim has Hepatitis C.

He pushed me to continue. I can't help but be honest with Denim; there is no poison to him, he is open and honest with me at all times, giving me no reason to ever lie to him, so I continued, "Sorry, I was going to say that I lost my dad to Hep C, but he was older and didn't take any care of himself and he became really sick. I didn't want to say that to you and freak you out."

"I'm fine Con, I'm on this new medication. I take one pill a day for three months and it's already kicked in. I spent the last year sick in bed and now I'm feeling everything coming back. I have energy and I'm getting up every day. It was the hardest year of my life, chronic fatigue turned into depression. When I met you, I had only just started to leave the house again."

I wanted to wrap him up in my arms, look after him forever. But I felt like he just wouldn't let me. We kept walking and we kept talking. He told me about a girl that he had met while I was away working, after meeting her he had gone over to her house. My heart was sinking but I'm smart enough to hide these feelings of rejection. A life of rarely getting what you want teaches you how to hide disappointment like the best of them.

But he told me there was nothing in it, that he had to explain to her that he wasn't interested in a relationship, he just wanted to focus on his health and his boys. Something about the way he was telling me what he told her, made me realise that the message was actually for me.

Always the gentleman, Denim walked me all the way home, I asked him if he wanted to come in for a beer and he responded, "I was hoping you'd say that."

I decided I'd give him one last chance to declare his undying feelings for me. That movie *He's Just Not That Into You* comes to mind, because he clearly wasn't.

We sat at my kitchen table, cracked another beer and continued chatting and I was like, fuck it, I'm bored of not knowing.

Even writing this, I can't help but be mad at myself, for not being able to just drop it, to just be grateful that he cares enough about me to be there, to laugh with me and protect me from my imaginary raping at the ATM.

But maybe, just maybe, I'm not as dumb as everyone thinks. Maybe, somewhere in my subconscious, I knew that I hadn't just met some guy who wanted to be friends. I was being reintroduced to a man that I've always loved, just never met.

So while sitting in my kitchen, on the bench, with the mood lights dimmed, applying another one of my mastermind high school tricks, I took a deep breath and I grabbed his hand, staring at him with my big irresistible hazel eyes… and he pulled away.

I cracked it, a mixture of embarrassed and over it. I stood up, told him I was tired and going to bed and that he had to leave. He looked hurt, I could see myself being a bitch to a man who had only ever been kind to me and my kids, but I was frustrated, I could see something there for us, but he couldn't see it.

And I was embarrassed. It made me feel desperate. I'm not fucking desperate. I'm the mother of four kids, I wrote an amazing book and bought myself a house; I'm pretty fucking fabulous.

But I didn't believe any of that and old feelings of hating my body came tumbling though my head. Anyone who has ever suffered an eating disorder will know that in any time of stress or crisis, no matter how "recovered" you are, you'll blame your weight.

I felt like a fat, unlovable, desperate loser as I pointed to the door and said the words, "Please leave". Which I fully understand only made me look like a bigger fuckwit.

Before leaving, Denim said, "Please don't give up on me."

I was astounded at his audacity. I felt anger burn though me and could almost see the reflection of flames in my own eyes. I've felt like that a few times, so angry that I had no idea what was going to stream out of my mouth and I responded, "How dare you? Do you know how long I have felt alone for? Do you know how long I've been unhappy for? I've paid my dues. I'm giving up on you, that's my right."

And he walked himself out.

While I locked up the house and went to bed a little heartbroken and a little jaded. I fell asleep but not before one final stab of immaturity, blocking Denim on Facebook.

I had a shit sleep. I always do when I'm drinking but especially if there is something on my mind. I woke up to a text message from someone who manages my public page.

She wrote: *This message came for you from Denim.*

The message read: *I do love you, more than you know. I'm sorry.*

We hung out one more time. I convinced him that I was cool with us just being friends, he believed me, I got a couple of wines into me and it ended in disaster; to the point that I yelled at him to get fucked from one end of the street to another and he stormed off.

Blocking people on Facebook rarely shows them the intended message of, "I don't care about you, I'm too mature to even be your mate." It kind of says, "I'm an immature fuckhead and I want to actively ignore you, by not ignoring you at all. Did you hear me? I'm ignoring you."

Real love can't be forced, or sped up; no short cuts or detours exist for real love. It takes its own divine course and you are just along for the ride.

FRIEND-ZONED

We weren't meant to be. It was obvious, and I had finally reached my limit. I can't be friends with someone I'm attracted to, not when my soul is telling me that we are supposed to be together, but I wanted to be around him so badly and I didn't want to lose him or his kids. And I didn't want my kids to lose them… so there was only one thing left to do.

I decided it was time to snap out of it.

I'm actually pretty good at snapping myself out of love; once I was head over heels in love with a guy who I found out was fucking someone else. I looked him cold in the eyes and said, "It doesn't matter what you say or do now, I've decided that I don't love you anymore."

And I didn't. No more sleepless nights; I was over him, flicked him like a switch, he even wrote me a message: *You threw me away like a dirty dishcloth.*

It's my superpower, one last gift from my dearly departed dad, a heart so broken that even when I think I'm in love, I can never be truly hurt by a man.

I explained to myself all of the reasons why Denim and I are actually more suited as friends; I don't need love right now, it's the last thing I need. My kids love him and romance would just fuck with us. I flicked the switch on Denim and it felt good. I felt like I was in control again.

I told him I was over it, I just wanted to be friends, and you could tell I was serious this time. I treated Denim like a friend and had genuinely gotten over my feelings for him. Denim was relieved. He didn't want to lose me and it was pretty obvious that we would lose each other on the path that we were going down.

Sometimes I do wish that we'd had a love at first sight connection, but we didn't. We had a complicated connection, but love is too grand to be trivialised with first sights.

One morning I woke up and everything was fucking up. All of my kids had been sick and just when I thought I was over the brunt of it, Arlo came down with a temperature that I just couldn't cut with any amount of Panadol or Nurofen.

After twelve months the book sales had slowed and my company had no money coming in. There was pressure for me to do some sponsored posts, or write a second book, or do public appearances; anything to get some cash through the door as we now had five staff members to pay. I just wanted to run away and hide. We'd needed all these staff members to run the business when the book was going crazy but now we didn't really need them anymore, but had to keep them. The pressure was building.

I took Billie-Violet to school, kept Arlo with me and asked Denim if he wanted to have brekkie with Arlo and me. He agreed. We went to our local cafe, ordered brekkie and I explained all of the things that were going wrong in my life. Denim just listened.

After brekkie, I made a doctor's appointment for Arlo and me: antibiotics for him, Valium for me. The appointment wasn't for an hour and a half, so Denim and I put Arlo, who was fading, in a supermarket trolley, took him to the chemist for some more pain relief and then for an ice cream.

The doctor's surgery is only up the road from me. The best thing about where I live is that we can walk everywhere we go – it's so nice to not be constantly getting in and out of a car, negotiating carparks.

Arlo got his antibiotics and surprisingly, the doctor agreed to giving me Valium. Apparently, thousands of haters revealing private details of my life and online stalking, mixed with running a company and raising four kids on your own, is actually stressful and it wasn't just in my mind.

Denim was waiting for me out the front and we pushed Arlo home together. I remember feeling like time stood still when Denim was around. He's calm, nothing stresses him out. He just takes my problems on board and workshops ways of handling them with me.

His kids came over after school and we all had dinner together – my two nannies, my four kids, Denim, his two kids and me. Like always at my house, there was plenty of dancing around the kitchen, music's always on, food is free-flowing and everyone's happy, the twins dress up and make us all laugh with their cute actions and outfits.

I remember looking at Denim. He seemed so happy and he told me he loved having his kids at my house, being surrounded by so much laughter and life. I took that as such a compliment. No matter how stressed I got, I never wanted my kids to grow up in a quiet or stiff environment. I just want wild hearts full of laughter, and music to tire them out until they fall asleep.

When all of the kids went to bed, Denim and I jumped on the couch; it was time to YouTube comedians, something we both loved doing, and we'd had a conversation earlier that day about some of our favourite skits. We then moved onto music,

YouTubing songs that meant the world to us. Denim played me a song that reminded him of his ex-wife, and I remember feeling grateful that we weren't romantically involved as he seemed kind of in love with her still.

I lay on his lap. You'd think I was pulling another sneaky high school test on the poor fucker, but I wasn't. I was fitting into my new role as his best friend and I was enjoying the security of it.

At one point, Denim's hand moved down and rested across my body onto my left breast; to this day he still claims it was an accident. Not having a bar of it, I defiantly asked him to move it, he seemed shocked and quickly pulled it away. Denim says that at that point, he realised that I'd been serious and I was over him.

Slowly, the glass of wine and Valium sucked me in and I fell asleep on Denim's lap on my couch. A comfortable place to rest an exhausted head.

Following the beautiful sleep that only Valium can bring me, I woke up peacefully in the morning, just before sunrise, and was shocked to find that my head was resting on top of Denim's bare chest. As a woman who had not slept on a man's chest in years, a woman who had felt so alone for so long, a woman whose stress levels had been through the roof and was carrying the weight of the world on her shoulders; in that split-second, I felt love in all of its warm glory.

I felt looked after, I felt like everything was going to be OK, I felt safe, I felt like drowning in the very moment. I pulled my head up and wiped my drool. Denim has the loveliest chest, and I almost didn't feel worthy of lying on it. I looked up at him and he was already looking down at me. With one hand he was holding my body, a bit of support so I didn't roll off the couch, and with the other, he stroked my hair and he smiled, just a good morning smile, an "I don't know either" kind of smile.

But then my defiance kicked back in and I leapt up to make tea. To show him that I didn't want a relationship, my pride wasn't going to let this man reject me again.

And that's what I did. I made brekkie for everyone. I made Billie-Violet's school lunch as Denim rolled his first smoke for the day and humbly sat down in my kitchen, watching me. He told me he was going home to get his kids to school – Denim's kids were twelve and sixteen, and he had flatmates, so he didn't need to be there with them during the night but wanted to make them brekkie, give them lunch money and see them off.

He told me he was coming back after that. And he did, and thus began another day of just the two of us, not leaving each other's side. Making excuses to stick to each other like glue. I was still sure that we were just friends, not letting myself believe anything else.

I told my nannies I was working so they would happily look after the kids for me. I grabbed my laptop and we drove down to the next town to a hippy shack-like sustainable venture full of yoga freaks and fisherman pants. I had previously started a blog for Denim – his own blog, somewhere he could write and express himself, which I was finding out was always a passion of his too.

We were back in time for school runs and I watched Billie-Violet ride her bike down the hill. That evening at my house, we repeated the previous night. Friends came over, we cooked up a Mexican feast, none of the kids asked any questions; they were all used to us by now. Two families were coming together and nobody even really noticed. We laughed; all we ever need to do is look at each other and we are laughing.

That night, we drank. I drank a beautiful pinot noir and Denim stuck with beer. Denim got the fire happening in my house as it was already starting to get cold.

I made beds in the lounge room for our kids, mattresses by the fire. And after a night of childrearing, dishes, lunches, drinking wine and sitting on the couch watching funny YouTube videos, I was ready for bed. There were still people up, my nannies and their friends, but the kids were drifting off.

I walked over to the stairs and said to Denim, "You can do whatever you want, sleep on the couch with your boys, or go home, or come up and sleep with me in my bed, I don't mind."

I've never seen Denim move with such certainty. He closed my laptop and before I could even hear him saying the words "your bed", he was already halfway up the stairs. It wasn't expected; I was actually quite surprised.

And so we went to bed together. I was there for one reason: to sleep. I took a Valium, jumped into my bed fully clothed, backed my arse into nuzzle at his waist, allowed myself to be spooned by his beautiful arms and drifted off to sleep. Only to be woken a few hours later with the biggest shock of my adult life: a pair of sweet lips pressed against mine.

"What are you doing?" I asked, a mixture of confusion and wanting to hear him say it. If I'm going to sleep with him, I know I'll fall for him and I want him to give me something tangible to hold onto and not just a "mates with benefits – fuck up my head" type of scenario.

To which Denim responded with, "Isn't it obvious that we are falling in love?"

This was the second time that day that I had heard those words. Earlier, a friend had said to me, "It's pretty obvious that you two are falling in love".

I had dismissed the words when they so thoughtlessly came out of her mouth, as she wasn't to know how hard I had tried to fall in love with him. But I couldn't ignore them from Denim. I grabbed his face and pulled it back into mine, licking his beautiful lips, feeling his tongue in my mouth. I was wearing a baggy white top, no bra and denim shorts, he put his hands up my top, as I instinctually sucked my belly right in and he grabbed my boob, pinching my nipple. I was trying to take it slow but my pussy was screaming at me to grab him and ram him inside me. Kissing my neck, pulling my hair, sucking my tits, finally he yanked my shorts and undies off and put his hand down inside me.

I lay there, biting my lip while our bodies were drawn towards each other. I pulled him close to me, his dick was so hard and I wrapped my legs around this man. This strong man whose one caring hand was holding my body close and the other was guiding him inside me, we were closer than we had ever been, face to face, on our sides, my arm under his neck. This moment right here. This is where I could die.

Be fun, be messy, invite people into your home, show the kids that you can laugh and stay up late on a school night every now and then.

Don't let friend-zoning get you down, there is always the possibility of a re-zoning.

THE SACRED FUCK OR SOLO FINGER TIME... SEX TALK

HAS A MAN EVER ASKED YOU IF HIS DICK SMELLS?

I wank. Who doesn't wank? We are just conditioned not to talk about it, and that is part of what is wrong with society, that's what stops us from owning our sexuality. It's what makes sex a chore. We aren't taught to teach anyone what we like because what we like has been hidden. If you can't pleasure yourself, how can a man pleasure you? If you don't talk about pleasuring yourself, how do you create a world where women's sexual pleasure is equally as important as men's?

But wanking is different. I've never been particularly assertive in my sexuality, I mean a man's orgasm feels like the goal, whereas a woman's feels like a bonus.

And all of the old insecurities came flooding back.

Do I feel fat?

Is my pussy in its best shape?

Let's be honest, I've had four kids and even though only two of them had travelled the route of the vagina, carrying the last two didn't exactly make it look better.

Once I was doing a live show in Edinburgh to a bunch of Queens and one of them, a newly separated Queen who later showed me a bunch of dick pics she'd received, got up and asked me, "How do you introduce a new dick into your life? I'm nervous."

I was like, "Hmm, I don't know. The new dick has never been my concern, it's my old vagina that I worry about."

Does it smell?

For fuck's sake, why are we always worried about the smell of our goddamn vaginas? Men like the smell of a healthy puss more then we like the smell of Dolce & Gabbana's latest fragrance. They'd move mountains to get a bit closer to that smell, yet there we are squirming, worried.

Is it hairy?

When was the last time I shaved?

I wonder if that was going through Denim's mind?

Does my dick smell?

Are my balls too hairy?

Is the fat patch above my dick too prominent for Con? Yep she's definitely thinking about my fat pad above my dick…

NO.

All he was thinking about was fucking me. Enjoying me. It kind of reminds me of the time I watched *Married at First Sight*, the man and the woman entering the experiment were interviewed beforehand and they were asked what their biggest fears or main concerns were.

Of course, the women said all of the relatable concerns, "I'm scared he won't like me, what if I'm not what he was expecting? I'm scared that he only likes really skinny chicks."

While the guy was voicing guy statements like, "I'm scared that I won't like her" and "What if she isn't what I ordered?"

Why are women so focused on being what men want, while men are so focused on getting what they want?

Your pussy smells beautiful, it's full of pheromones and all things sexy.

Pubic hair doesn't bite. You don't want to be with a man who's scared of it... Now who's the pussy?

Relax, the sexiest thing you can do is realise how sexy you are and lose yourself in sex.

WHAAAAT? GIRLS WANK?

When I was a kid, I was a creep. You know, like when you hear your kids go quiet in the bathtub, so you run in there to make sure that one isn't doing something disgusting to the other? Like the time I didn't know I was on loudspeaker and my sister was in a clothes shop and when she asked me how my day was, and I responded, "Fucked! The kids had to come inside coz I caught them shovelling sand up their bums in the backyard."

She quickly took me off loudspeaker, only the shop assistant cracked up and said, "Tell her I have kids, I know all about it."

I was the first to get my clothes off and show my mates I had discovered some new flap of skin in my fanny. My mates and I had no idea what our clitorises were, so we nicknamed them our "capsicums", which is kind of cute considering if you didn't know what a capsicum was and just saw it from the outside, you'd be pleasantly surprised to see the magic within.

That creepy-kid side of me never stopped flourishing. I loved stealing porn off whoever, my neighbours, friend's dads, looking at the inside of a vagina with a throbbing dick near it made me crack up laughing and I was secretly so intrigued. I was like, "Grooooooosssss! Show me another one!"

My only saving grace was that I didn't have Google back then, and without the power to un-see forbidden images, I can only imagine the strain on my brain from where my curiosity would have taken me.

I remember the first time I masturbated – I was twelve. I had no idea what I was doing. They taught us what masturbation was, but they didn't teach you how. Female masturbation was such a taboo topic when I was a kid that I honestly thought I was just fucking around with my capsicum.

I used to move my hand on and off my vag, and after shaking it around for about four minutes, the pressure would build up until something would happen and I had to stop. It was fun, but didn't feel amazing or even great; it was just different. I suppose my sexual organs were still developing coz these days, I fucking love a good orgasmatron.

I told my best friend and we decided to do it together. We told our other friend, and she admitted she was doing the same thing. It turned out all the kids were doing it. And then we realised that we were actually having a wank. How strange.

For about a year, I proceeded to enjoy the old finger bang. I used to think about the images I had stored in my head from pornos I had sneaked a peek of. I still remember them today, now that's a solid wank bank with great returns.

Something happened to me in my teenage years. I went from being the most confident kid on earth to being a really, really unconfident teenager. I went from being very popular to being quite unpopular. I heard the words "you're too much" more than anything else as a teenager.

And I was. The problem was that I craved attention so badly, I'd become even more loud, more in your face, more "too much" and face more rejection. I became confused; I was a good person who was suffering a lot. I wanted a boyfriend so badly; I see it in teenagers now, they would do anything a boy told them to do, just for some godforsaken attention.

My growing sexuality reflected that. Sometimes, I'd think about really weird things, men that I didn't find attractive at all, like old men, overweight ones, bald ones... I had no idea why I was turned on by the idea of sleeping with these guys; guys that I'd never actually sleep with, or look twice at as a superficial teenager.

I remember the first time I was ever actually turned on by something in real life and not just in my head or with my hand. I went on a double date to the movies and we saw the film *Twister*, remember that? I think I was about twelve or thirteen. We all went up to the back of the cinema, I'm pretty sure it was pre-rehearsed. I really liked the guy, he was cute as fuck, dark-skinned and kind, and we were an "item". We hadn't had a conversation but we were together, OK?

I remember the bra thing I was wearing, it was like a sports bra, crop top thing with strawberries on it; it made me feel so grown up. Do you remember that stage where everyone was wearing Mr Man tops? Like they'd say "Mr Lazy" or "Mr Grumpy" or some shit, really intended for kids, but grungy teenagers deemed them appropriate too. I was wearing one of them and a denim skirt and a pair of purple suede Doc Martins, coz let's face it, for a frizzy-haired chubby teenager with more eyeliner than Amy Winehouse, I was cool as fuck.

So there we were, in the back row. He looked at me, licked his lips and went in for the pash. We pashed and pashed. He put his hands all over me, naturally I sucked in my stomach. His hands grabbed my boobs; I was so excited I wanted to stay in that moment forever and ever.

But after about fifteen minutes of pashing, the teenage dream/adult's worst nightmare, the most dreaded thing happened: I got my period. I felt it trickling out and dripping onto my undies. I excused myself, got up, shimmied my denim skirt down and went to the toilet. About to do the old rolled-up toilet paper and sit on my feet for the rest of the movie so blood doesn't get on the seat, pulled my undies down and... whaaaat?

Nothing. Well, something, but no period. It was clear. I had no idea what it was but wasn't worried. I had been taught about all kinds of discharge in primary-school health classes and pissed myself laughing, reminding my friends all the time, using the words at every opportunity, "Miss, do you mind if I discharge myself early from class? I have a doctor's appointment." "I love this cake, it's sooo moist."

So I went back to lover boy and continued to passionately kiss while Helen Hunt freaked out over the world's worst tornados, only for it to happen again. I noticed that there was a direct link to the wetness of my vagina and this guy's hands all over my body. Weird. I didn't know what lube was or what my body was preparing myself for; all I knew was that my vagina was responding to this guy in bizarre ways.

He broke up with me the following week. Actually, he upgraded. She looked a hell of a lot like me, was a bit smarter, a bit skinnier and a bit quieter, way less funny. You can't have it all, fuckface.

And he doesn't even know that he went down in history as the first man I'd crack a slippery over. Almost twenty years later, I finally slept with him. They always come back.

It wasn't worth the wait.

Pussy pride. It's time to break free and end the stigma that women don't masturbate; this plays into the ideology that sexual pleasure is reserved for men. If more people spoke about, and opened up about females wanking, the message would be clearer. We are here to fulfil our needs as much as yours. And maybe we can all look forward to a day where men don't roll over after jizzing on our tummies and start snoring, leaving us to have a silent wank next to them.

Start with your friends: ask them how often they masturbate, ask the horny bitches if their husbands know. Let's start talking

THE FIRST IS THE WORST

I met Darren on a train one night. He was dreadlocked, ultra-cool, skated, and was a graffiti artist, which where I'm from was cool. At the time. To me.

Beggars can't be choosers, OK?

I was fourteen – that's right guys, fourteen. I used to always tell people that I was sixteen, because losing your virginity at fourteen sounds bad in certain circles. I have learnt so much in the last five years about sex; what's expected of women sexually and what society portrays a women's sexuality to look like, versus what it actually is.

I had been fingered – you know why I love the word fingered? Coz I know you hate it, I feel you cringe. Denim even hates it, so I'm constantly asking for a fingering. He is so grossed out and the grosser he finds it, the more I love it. Told you I'm a creep!

But that was as far as I had gone… for myself. I had of course given head and handjobs; sex was swiftly becoming a "giving" sport. In a group of ten girlfriends, half of them had already had sex. So, I didn't feel like I was being particularly adventurous.

I went out with him for around two weeks before it was time. Two weeks for me is a long time – I was planning the underage wedding. He was seventeen and had made it very clear that we should fuck – it would "strengthen us". He told me that he loved me and couldn't believe how lucky he was that we had met. I actually think he was on an E when he said those things. I had no experience with ecstasy, so I just couldn't believe how much he loved me. He even wrote my name in a "piece" that he painted. Any graffiti moles out there will know that a piece is a big 3D word that takes hours and it is illegally painted at a train station or wall of a supermarket. Unfortunately for my popularity, the piece was slashed (an anonymous line painted through it, the ultimate stab towards the artist) and my name was also slashed. It's incredible how you can be dissed as a graffiti artist when you're not even a graffiti artist. My unpopularity was pushing boundaries.

A week after the Ecstasy night, I was staying at one of my friend's houses and he came over. Somehow, he had managed to convince all of my friends to sleep in the other room and give us my mate's bed. I wasn't planning on doing it, I don't even know how I ended up doing it, I wasn't even drunk. But he'd convinced me I'd love it.

"It's the best feeling, better then drugs." (Hmm. I hadn't tried drugs yet, but I loved a good old finger bang and he conveniently had a condom.)

First he went down… like down, down. I was shocked. He put his head between my legs and started to lick the inside of my vagina…

WHAAAAAAAT??????

That was his way of getting me into the mood. The thing about headjobs is that you need to be 100% comfortable to enjoy them. If you have any doubts about the shape, or smell, or taste, or what you are supposed to be doing then *bam*, you aren't happy. The poor guy probably thought that a girl's sexual response going to be the same as a bloke's – put it in your mouth and voilà, you cum.

I became so uncomfortable that I made the decision that if he ever came up (it felt like it was taking forever) I'd never let him go back there. I'll just be a giver. I'll have sex to fulfil his needs and to get a boyfriend. I will give myself pleasure; I don't want to impose my sexuality on boys when I'm quite happy just to give. Anything beats this self-consciousness that I'm feeling now, cringing away while he works his little heart out down there.

I just lay there with a squished-up cringe-face, wondering if I was doing what I was supposed to be doing, when he finally came up and kissed me. He thought I was panting in pleasure, I was actually having a panic attack over the thought of my vag in someone's mouth. Whose idea was it to lose my virginity sober?

He unrolled the condom and I think what followed were thirty of the most uninspiring, yet painful, seconds of my life. I considered asking him to stop, it hurt so much, but he was in a world of his own, I could have been anyone, his hand, his mate's, there was no connection. He stared at the pillow to complete his mission.

And then we lay there, I was filled with adrenaline, because I was now a woman and he was trying to convince me that time speeds up when you have sex, because he was the expert and all: "It's funny how time speeds up. That would have felt like a minute but we were actually fucking for half an hour."

Right – cool story, bro.

Now that we were a consummated legit couple, I could let him know how deeply in love with him I was. I even wrote him a poem, because if there is one thing teenage boys love, it must be poems. And within three days of my virginity being swept away, I was dumped.

Yep, dumped. At a train station, no less.

I wonder if every time a kid got dumped at a train station, they wrote their story of love and despair on the chairs, people might stop dumping each other there. I got on a train and sobbed. My poor little heart ached, it thought this was my forever man, I thought we would have babies and get married and tell our grandkids that he was my first and we had been in love since I was fourteen. A woman walked over to me, puffy-faced and going for gold with my ugly crying, and just before she got off, she said, "Baby, I don't know you, but I know he isn't worth it." And of course, twenty years later I can vouch for that. Even if at the time I was devastated.

Sex got better, but it never got great. I learnt something my twenties: I had a sexual revelation while watching Oprah (God I owe that woman). She was interviewing a woman who said that sexually, men like to desire what they are looking at, but women like to feel desired. She explained that nothing turns women on like being desired. It all made sense to me, that's why I fantasised over things that wouldn't usually turn me on, men who were too old for me or men for who I was, for lack of a better phrase, out of their league, because it made me feel desired and that turned me on. To feel sexy and wanted, and needed, and lusted over... how sexy is that?

But now I understood my sexuality and what turned me on, I wanted to change it. Why? Because it's so needy. It's so dependent on being accepted by a male's perception of sexy – it's not about owning your own desires. I want to want something without always caring if I'm doing it for them, or what they think of me. I want it to not matter to me while I get lost in my own pleasure. And I'm working on it.

Can we just teach our boys one thing? Fucking her under false pretences of a relationship is deceitful. Be honest. If you still get a root... Bravo son. If you don't, it wasn't yours to begin with.

Can we teach our girls a few things? Starting with, stop fucking dickheads just because they skate. And sex is about you *both* getting off, connecting and respecting each other... At least if you get off, you won't feel as used when he turns out to be an A-grade dickhead. And sex doesn't even begin to get good until you get over your paranoia of your own body. Your body is perfect, you are absolutely perfect, enjoy being so fucking perfect.

And it does get better, I promise you it gets better and there is nothing wrong with you for not enjoying it... Aunty Con didn't either, nor did most of your friends, even the ones who spoke of multiple orgasms on her first time – she probably hated it the most. And one day you will meet someone who gets you off so hard and you won't be able to keep your hands off him (or her), I promise.

THE SCARY WORLD OF
KIDS, SEX AND PORN

But I still worry. I worry about our kids, it really scares me.

Back in my day, well, yeah that makes me sound old and fucked, but the truth is that in my day, sex was dominated by boys. They spoke about us like we were objects, discussing who smells like what, who goes on top, who goes down. The sexual partnership, instead of being between a boy and a girl, was between a boy and his mates. And today? It's gotten so much worse.

I read an article and it terrified me. It was published on www.fightthenewdrug.org. It taught me all about the secret world of today's teenagers that we have no idea about. A survey commissioned by Plan Australia and Our Watch gathered answers from 600 young Australians between the ages of fifteen and nineteen about their sex lives.

"Don't Send Me that Pic" is the name of the survey. This digital age of dick pics, easily shared information and porn at your fingertips has made sexual harassment a normal part of a young girl's day-to-day life. These young minds aren't old enough to understand the difference between reality and fiction. Have you watched porn lately? It's all anal, cream-pie, group and bizarre objects; there isn't any human involvement anymore. It's just a male's wonderland.

And young girls are paying the price.

These scenes inspire their first sexual experiences, and they are being pressured into re-enacting things that they don't want to do. Girls are considering themselves mere tools in boy's sexual adventures, rating the sex based on how happy he seems to be with it.

When asked, "How do you know if a boy likes you?" an eighth grader responded: "He still wants to talk to you after giving him oral sex."

Boys who were taught by today's porn are teaching girls how to have sex. Girls are reporting the constant pestering by boys to provide naked pics, and despite not wanting to send them, they feel it's the norm now, and unavoidable.

Girl's bodies are being ranked and compared to those of porn stars and it is leaving them insecure. Genital surgery has increased threefold in the last decade in young women 15–24 years old. This I can understand; the last time I watched porn, I was wondering why their vaginas looked like smooth, skinny, little fairy fannies, and mine looks like a fat elephant's ear.

If girls don't wax all of their pubes off, the other kids consider them gross and dirty. I've almost given up my pube fight, I feel like they have been gone too long. I feel like advocating for the pure pussy, like a 95-year-old bald man looking in the mirror every day wondering if today's the day that one might sprout back.

There is physical injury from porn-inspired sex acts. Yep, you read that right. Because when someone tries to put his dick in my arse, I can pull it out and tell the little creep he's hurting me; but hey, my sex life isn't being discussed all over a schoolyard that literally seems like my whole world; that would be terrifying, and I might grin and bear it too, if I was fifteen.

The director of the Domestic Violence Prevention Centre on the Gold Coast wrote this about the increase of porn-related sex injuries to girls aged fourteen and up: "In the past few years we have had a huge increase in intimate partner rape of women from 14 to 80+, and the biggest common denominator being porn consumption." [1]

Porn is only ever OK for people old enough and mature enough to distinguish between fantasy and reality.

Girls need to be taught the clear lines between loving, consensual sex and re-enacted porn aimed to only satisfy boys.

All teenagers need to be taught that sex is between two people. Talking about your insecurities with your friends is great, laughing about a sexual experience with your friends is cruel.

---

1 Sourced from **www.collectiveshout.org/**

WHAT DOES THE FUTURE BRING?

Are you scared yet?

Because I am terrified for my daughters, for my sons. What's scarier? Raising a girl who becomes a victim, or a boy who becomes a perpetrator? Because the odds aren't good in this day and age.

How do we slow this down? How do we teach girls that they need to own their own sexuality? How do we teach them it's not about porn or getting a guy off; it's about two people with one common denominator: they respect each other?

I suppose that was my first concern with teaching teenagers how to enjoy sex, how to own their sex life, and not fall victim to the things that I'd fallen victim to. But to really get some solid advice instead of just drawing on personal experience, I've grabbed the expertise of the amazing sexologist, Dr Nikki Goldstein.

We have read a lot about young girls today feeling like sex is something they "give" not something they love. How can we teach them to own their sexuality from a young age?

It starts with the terminology we use and what we tell them about sexual pleasure. One great one is changing how we discuss virginity. We still speak as though we lose something, hence the term "losing your virginity". As some women can break their hymen during sporting activities or in other ways before they have sex, they don't actually lose anything, they experience something for the first time. Some people will say virginity is a special gift or flower to give away, but it's not. It's an amazing experience that someone has at a certain time in their life. We also need to incorporate sexual pleasure into education for younger girls. Often we will talk about periods and babies and how to be protected during sex, but we don't talk about sex feeling good, especially for women. We discuss masturbation for boys but we also need to talk about this for women too. What it is, how it feels good and what some of the benefits are. Even discussing the clitoris can help women to shift their mind. If as many as 80% of women are experiencing orgasms through clitoral stimulation, why don't we talk about that too with younger women? Is it because the clitoris is not involved in making a baby? When we leave information like this out, it teaches women that their sexuality is about penetration and procreation. It's a matter of normalising topics but also introducing language and certain topics at a younger age.

How can we make sure our kids aren't learning too much from porn? It's so accessible and derogatory towards women and they are so young and impressionable.

We really can't stop kids looking at porn. We can try but even our attempts at trying can send a negative message and make it more exciting, because it becomes more taboo. You might be banning the internet at home, or putting blockers on and searching through history, but I even worry that it starts to say that porn is taboo, so it's exciting to go and search it. I also worry that in future relationships, men will be more likely to hide their porn usage and women will also have negative beliefs around it if it's desired or even if they desire it. There might be guilt because as younger kids they were so strongly taught that porn was wrong. I'm not suggesting that kids watching porn is OK, however great attempts to block it can also send a negative message to them as future sexual adults.

Not all porn is bad, but it isn't helpful to have kids learn from porn. The reason many kids look at porn is because they are curious about sex and what it looks like. They learn from porn when they don't have any other adequate resources to look at. This is why it's important to counterbalance the negative influences of porn. Have those conversations about sex, sexual pleasure and even porn from a younger age. Make sure you send the message that there are open channels of communication around sex and that they can come to you with any questions. Discuss porn and ask kids if they have seen anything and if they have any questions about what they saw. It's important to make it known that they are not in trouble but rather it's good to be able to discuss their thoughts and feelings around it. Giving them adequate forms of sexual education can also help. You might want to find some resources online that talk to kids about sex so they have the answers that they might have been looking for online. The biggest issues to discuss with porn are around respect for women, realism of the acts performed and how porn is just like a sexy movie, and also the expectations they feel they have after seeing porn or even hearing of others watching it.

Do you have any advice on parenting young people during their sexual beginnings? Bearing in mind that they think we are a bunch of fuckwit losers who make them cringe if we so much as bring it up.

The biggest thing is to make sure they can discuss anything with you. You might not have all the answers and you can be honest with your kids about that. Sex can be wonderful but also complex and sometimes scary. I think kids should be turning to their parents for help and advice around sex, but it really is up to a parent to make that known to them, to give them the permission. Sometimes getting on their level might mean using the language that they use and also discussing topics that are relevant. Giving kids condoms is always a good start and discussing how they are used. It used to be that you gave kids condoms when they started dating someone and were over the age of 16, but they might be too late and as scary as that sounds, it's better for them to be protected and understand how to use condoms and also that they have the right to.

Teach our girls that your virginity isn't losing something, or giving something away. It's the beginning of discovering what could be (should be) a life full of another pleasure, like food, Netflix and now sex.

Not all porn is bad; some of it respectful and healthy. As long as people know that just like a movie, it isn't real; special effects and camera tricks are used.

Take away the taboo and mystery around sex and your frisky little shits might be less inclined to look at porn from such a young age.

The most important lesson girls and boys need to be taught around sex and porn is the importance of respecting the woman. Porn doesn't always demonstrate this.

Keep sex open, a light and easy conversation (sounds like a diet plan) between you and the teenagers. Make sure they know they can tell you *anything*... then wait until they are out of the room before you start rocking and shaking and vomiting over yourself.

CAN YOU JUST BLOW NOW? EXPERT ADVICE ON LONG-TERM RELATIONSHIP SEX

To me, sex is a huge part of feminism. Owning your sexuality shows the world that it ain't for sale. I guess first of all you should ask yourself one important question: are you enjoying your sex life? I mean, are you orgasming? Masturbating? Initiating a fuck with your fella? Or are you cringing at the thought, getting it over and done with, making excuses...

If it's the latter, please listen to this next sentence.

IT'S NOT YOUR FAULT.

But it doesn't mean that it's not your *responsibility*.

I read an article by Marian Meade where she said: "Intimacy is the glue that holds relationships together." For some reason, I was never able to forget that. Are we just intimate people who need to be touched and held and kissed? I'm not even just talking about sex – intimacy can be everything from kindness to non-sexual physical touch, to a quick hard fuck in the back of a car. It's all intimacy, and when I heard the word "glue", I realised that intimacy is that bit of magic between two people; it's the reason that when I'm at a party, there could be fifty people in a room but I'll pick up on my lover's mood; or that deep-seated knowledge that no matter how far apart you are, you are always, in a roundabout way, coming home to each other. Intimacy gives you the ability to look across the room and ask someone if they are OK, comfortable or if they want to go home. All with just your eyes. That's glue. So without intimacy, how can we be expected to want to have sex?

Do you know how common sexless relationships are? If couples have sex less than ten times a year, it is considered sexless; so many of my friends fall into this category and I have before too.

So why? Why don't we want to root?

I wrote this blog after interviewing Dr Nikki Goldstein for the first time:

Lately I've interviewed a couple of people about sex.

In particular, women's sex drive in long-term relationships really interests me.

I spoke to the divine sex doctor, Dr Nikki Goldstein, about why we lose interest and would prefer to have a cup of tea or eat toast than to have the man we love get us off.

First thing I have learnt is the average sex drive varies greatly. The average amount a couple fucks is between once a week to once a month.

But we only hear from people who brag about how much sex they are having; those who don't have much at all tend to shy away from that fact, making us feel abnormal if we aren't swinging from the ceiling shouting, "harder, motherfucker!"

Second, the average is declining and I think that's due to women's workloads having increased. Today, women

are spending on average 30% more time with their children then they did thirty years ago. We also now work.

But the main reason Dr Nikki told me she hears time and time again, and I can't get it out of my head, is this one sentence: "You don't consider me."

Who the fuck wants to root a bloke that hasn't considered them??? When someone leaves muddy footprints on the floor you just swept, or comes back from work before you but doesn't put dinner on, or slept in while you did the school run?

Not me. You can stick to wanking, and so will I.

Another problem is the lack of importance put on the female orgasm. I saw a sex therapist say, "A women not cumming is like both of you getting dressed up for an amazing day out, you get on the train, it stops at the place... but only he gets out."

Dr Nikki Goldstein told me that "after play" is the answer; sex is often considered over when the man ejaculates his holy love syrup, rolls over and goes to sleep...

Up ya get boys, guess what? It's not all about you. Fingers, mouths and sex toys are the way of the future; I know it's hard to accept but the glorious penis rarely finishes the job.

And finally, I will leave you with this piece of wisdom Steve Biddulph (*Raising Boys*) told me when I interviewed him: "Every second of a marriage is a kind of a dance. You are two people dancing. And if that ends up in bed, it just means the dance was going especially well!"

So what Steve is really saying is everything is foreplay. **Remember that, blokes. Help us, give us some non-sexual physical touch and, above all, consider us. Because**

what you do out of the bedroom is going to impact what we do in it.

*

Let's be honest, an orgasm is the destination. I'm so tired of hearing people say it's about the journey and not about the destination. It's fucking not. I have a three-hour drive to my nearest city and, fuck my life, it bores the crap out of me. I don't even look out the window. If Denim's driving, I try to sleep. That's about how interested I am in the journey. If I'm not going to reach orgasm… well, if you don't mind… I think I'll sleep through this.

It took me a long time to master this; the first thing I had to do was stop faking my orgasms. Why do we do this, ladies? Not only do men get to fuck us and have a piece of the sweet, sweet nectar, they get to orgasm and the icing on the cake is that they get to walk off feeling like the biggest hero on earth because they made you cum.

Which we all know is soooooooo hard to do when statistics have proven that only 20% of all women orgasm vaginally; blokes think they are just the biggest stallions because they are making every women orgasm, despite these odds being stacked so heavily against them.

Boys… we have been faking it. In fact, if any of my exes are reading this and you fucked me with your penis and no other stimulation with your hand or tongue? Chances are I faked it and you believed it. We both suck.

Bring on the destination! And if you can't get there with a penis or his fingers, invest in some sex toys; nothing makes you cum quicker than a vibrator. Imagine if you knew that every time you had sex, you were going to have an orgasm? That migraine might miraculously vanish. And while I'm ranting, do you know what else I'm fucking over? Women's sex lives being controlled by the male ego. Like, "No, we can't use toys coz it will offend my husband. I wouldn't even suggest it." Shut up, just shut up. I don't see any blokes sacrificing their orgasms for our egos. In fact, I think we will all have a lot more fun if we leave our egos outside the bedroom.

Tips to improve your sex life

1) Intimacy, non-sexual physical touch, consider each other, kindness. Tell him he needs to help you to get in the mood, just like he likes the shaft of his nob rammed down your throat until you want to spew on him; you like the dishes being done, the sheets being changed, a fucking glass of pinot in the bath.

2) Fake it until you make it (actually, this is my life motto on everything, not just sex. Well, everything except your orgasm). Even if you're not in the mood, do it. It will get you in the mood. Sometimes when we have had a long break from sex (replaced with Netflix and online stalking of exes) we start to cringe at the idea of it; we fall out of the loop. By just jumping in the deep end and getting back on the horse with little thought, the attraction grows, the respect grows, the relationship heals, and the sexual connection strengthens. Before you know it, you're swinging from the lights while he spanks you with the broomstick.

3) Demand that orgasm. Teach him. I know it feels awkward but it's about time we all get off. Sex is about all sorts of touching and kissing and licking, it's not just about penetrating and banging away until one person comes and the other pops another Xanax.

4) And, here is the key: lower your expectations. Not everybody is happy with their sex lives. Everyone thinks everyone else is having these crazy sex lives, where they roll around and change positions and role-play and get all sweaty and finger each other's bums. They aren't. They just aren't. Well, maybe swingers and porn stars are.

*

Me and Denzy? Denim was the first man I got lost in. Sex to him isn't just getting off, it's rated purely on how hard he can make me cum. When we first met he would ask me questions, "Is this good? Is this where you like to be touched?" He never just dicked me, shoving it in and hoping some Ecstasy fell out the end of it, doing all the work for him. He was always looking at me, waiting for a reaction, trying something else, refusing to cum until I did.

Someone has taught this man how to fuck and I am not even jealous, just grateful. His hands are constantly on me; sex isn't sex without clitoral stimulation.

Denim has the most beautiful hands: everything he does with them, sexual and nonsexual, is done with care. From just stroking his kids' hair, to handing me a plate, he'll brush his hand on me, always giving a reassuring safety with his strong hands.

He will start kissing my tits, moving down to my stomach and I'll jerk him up, "Babe I haven't had a shower and it's been a big day, just stay up here" to which he will respond "It's me," and insists on going down. Somehow, "It's me" are the sexiest words I have ever heard.

And that kind of sums up our sex life: it's him. He makes me feel sexy no matter what state I'm in. My sexuality is so important to him. I can be lazy or unshaven, or have morning breath... and... it's him, so I'm still sexy.

Lying on his chest, looking down at his body, I can't believe I've found him. I can't believe he loves me. He is the sexiest man I've ever seen and I feel like we could be one. He once whispered to me, "You know I've dreamt this? I've dreamt this sex and I've dreamt your body, I've dreamt you before I met you." And I was transformed. I'm not the matted hair, short flabby girl with vaginal insecurities, I'm a woman, a sexy one that's travelled from lifetime to lifetime to connect with this man.

And then there is the lazy sex. The everyday sex, where we barely change positions, usually lying on our sides and most of our clothes still on because we only have a minute to ourselves, and it makes us closer. Don't ever think you have a shit sex life if you're having sex with someone you love. It ain't shit.

Now I think it's time for a wank break. Stop reading, have a masti and come back refreshed.

Intimacy is the glue. You need to keep working on it.

"You don't consider me" and therefore I will not fuck you. It's pretty simple: wash the clothes and make some meals. Make my life easier and I'll feel like banging you. Even the least selfish people in the world are behaving selfishly when they are lazy.

Non-sexual physical contact is like human lube.

Gotta start somewhere – start today. Demand Your Orgasm, have I said that enough? Do you get the message? I want to see you cum baby!!!

Lower your expectations. We can all have shit sex, and sometimes only some of us enjoy it.

RAISING YOUR TRIBE

WHAT IF THE WHINGING, CHAOS AND FIGHTING IS ACTUALLY ALL OK?

The co-founder of Rafiki Mwema, Anne Marie, was holding a fundraiser in Perth, and staying at a local hotel with a swimming pool; so the kids and I went to visit her, and to sneak into the pool.

The kids were jumping off the islands and I was half talking to Anne Marie, and half watching the kids – "Mum, watch this!!" – and as I make a huge deal over a ridiculously unco bellyflop, Anne Marie turned to me and said, "You're such a good mum, Con."

I was grateful, but guilty. What Anne Marie didn't know about was all the fights my kids had had that day: the screaming, the tantrums; it's relentless. My kids are so badly behaved all of the time and because I'm not a smacker, I find myself just yelling back to gain control and we all end up looking like a circus.

"I don't feel like a good mum," I told her. "I lose my temper constantly, the kids are out of control and just when I think everyone is finally going to behave, one pinches the other and it's fucking on. Don't get me started with car drives. Jesus Christ, I bribe them with shit from the servo and make them promise to behave, and five minutes later, I'm threatening to throw it out of the car window. When I fall asleep at night, I wonder how the hell I'm going to wake up in the morning and do it all over again."

Anne Marie responded in a way that has changed my outlook on my children and myself. "Babies cry, that's how they communicate; toddlers whinge, that's how they communicate; teenagers complain, that's how they communicate; and mums... well, mums say "for fuck's sake" under their breath before even responding every time. That's how we communicate and survive. But guess what, Con? It's all a hell of a lot better than silence. A house full of whinging toddlers and fighting kids and parents, exhausted by the millions of questions and requests that their children are throwing at them, is a healthy one.

"I work with children who have been through trauma and when I walk into a house and see bad behaviour, outbursts and food being thrown around I think, 'Good, I can see this behaviour they are showing me' and I can work with it. It's when I walk into a house with silent children, scared toddlers, children who don't come home and parents who aren't communicating with their children, that I worry.

"You often see children behaving particularly badly when their mums are around. Terrible, right? Like they don't like or respect you? Or you give into them too much, and everyone is right, you are a pushover? Right? Wrong. You are the person that your children have the strongest connection with – that makes you their safety line. Little kids in a big world put on a brave front all day; kids might be mean to them, the teacher made them nervous, they didn't feel like their work was good enough and they hold it in because they don't feel safe enough to let go of their emotions. The minute they see their mums walking towards them, they feel that safety flood over them again and they can release their emotions, emotions that they often can't control, as the front cortex in their brains isn't fully developed, allowing

258

them to understand and process these emotions properly.

"So instead of thinking of yourself as a bad mum because your children's behaviour is worse when you're around, think of yourself as a great mum whose child feels safe and connected when you are around."

Anne Marie has taught me so much about children and their behaviour; she has taught me that childhood is about attachments: bringing up kids who attach and connect easily to you, to teachers and other kids; and it's about communication: loud and hectic households full of love are normal and fine. Communication comes in so many forms.

She has taught me to believe in myself as a mum, that everything is going to be OK. Sometimes I think that parenthood is 50% raising kids and 50% learning to believe in yourself as a good person who can raise good kids.

Screaming can be ignored but silence must always be broken.

We all lose our shit.

All kids are completely fucked at times, sometimes all at once; it's called super fucked.

Chaotic screams and tears and complaints are just fine.

Watch out for the quiet ones, the ones who are trying to disappear; they are usually trying to hide something and it can be confused with "good behaviour."

Just love them, communicate with them, be open with them, say sorry when you were too short and hug them and kiss them after fights.

You can't ruin anything with love.

STEP-PARENTING: TAKING THEM INTO YOUR HEART WHEN THEY DIDN'T COME FROM YOUR TUMMY

I'd love to lie. I really would. In fact, I've lied before, but the truth is that step-parenting is no walk in the park.

Remember that movie *Stepmom*? Where Julia Roberts says "fuck" a few times, hires a hot model to make the kid's schoolmates jealous and they have a bonding singalong in the car, followed by some approving and hopeful gazes? The biological mother dies and everyone lives happily ever after? Yeah, well… it's nothing like that.

One of the hardest parts of leaving a marriage with kids is knowing that nobody else will ever love your kids as much as you do, and even if your partner isn't your cup of tea anymore, chances are that they love your kids a hell of a lot more than "Frankie, 1km away, loves tits" on Tinder is ever gonna.

On one hand I'm all, "Fuck everyone! Step-parenting is a privilege! He's lucky to be blessed with a woman who has kids; it's a bonus."

On the other hand, I'm like, "Fuck this. It's bloody hard and while it's rewarding long-term, it's thankless in the short term."

I am not an expert – how many times have I said that in this book? Do you get it, Queens? I'm not an expert on *anything*. But I have my experience, and that of those that I love, so here is my advice.

Leave the disciplining to the biological parent

The most common mistake I see in new step-parenting relationships is when the biological parent shares responsibilities with the step-parent, so the step-parent assumes that equates to shared disciplinary roles.

The truth is that a step-parent needs to be a friend first. They have years and years of trust to make up for before they can start disciplining their stepchild. Most children of divorced parents already have two parents, who are often fighting over them. What they need is a friend, someone on their side to have their back and create some fun.

I can go off at my kids; in fact, I do quite often. Do you know how scared they are of me when I start yelling? They don't flinch because they trust me, they know I'll calm down, and I'm not really cancelling Christmas because one threw a cup of Milo on the other and I now have to clean it up. That kind of trust took years of empty threats and shit parenting to build.

Now, if I did that to a friend's kid? Yelled at them and told them that I'm cancelling Christmas? They'd be devastated. It wouldn't be fair and I wouldn't do it.

Dr Phil says that if a parent isn't involved before the age of four or five, then they should never take on a primary disciplinary role parenting the children. Your job is to support the biological parent's decisions and stand by them, but he says you will never be mum or dad; you will always be a partner the parent has brought in to the family.

Friendship first.

Ironically, when you talk about parenting, it's a given that in most households, women are the more hands-on parent (I'm not being a man-hater, it's just a fucking fact and we need to be able to talk about facts without offending the goddamn universe). When it comes to step-parenting, it's more common for men to have a larger role; because in a divorce, it's still more common for the mother to be the primary caregiver, which in turn means that when a man enters a family, he will usually be joining a family with kids in it almost full-time. However, when a woman joins a family, it will usually have children in it only part-time.

This can create a few problems. First, men are less patient then women. I have no studies to back that up, but in my experiences (with friends and family), I have found that other people's kids annoy men more than women.

Mothers often feel torn between their kids, who she just wants to crumble for, and her partner, who thinks she gives into them too much. This has been my experience.

Denim thinks I'm too soft; in fact, that is the main thing we argue over. He isn't patient enough with my children and I won't back down and be harder on them because I believe in gentle parenting. I don't believe my kids should be judged on bad behaviour; they come from a huge family and getting a tiny bit of attention requires so much fighting, and yelling, and acting out, that I just don't blame them. I judge them on their intentions, which are always pretty spot on to me.

Be realistic about expectations

When we are talking about a blended family, you can end up with a father who worships his own kids, because they only come once a week (or fortnight) but treats yours with less love and respect. It's a natural occurrence and it happens all the time.

It's upsetting for the kids and, which any mum will tell you, is also hurtful for her; we feel what our kids feel. Now I understand this, I understand it all. It can be much easier to forgive your biological kids; however when a stepkid fucks up it can grind on you, especially when your partner is looking at them with rose-coloured glasses. It's frustrating and it takes a long time for you to start wearing those same rose-coloured glasses, especially when children and their parents have a secret bond. It can feel like an exclusive club to anyone who is on the outside.

Children who come from a broken family often have one thing in common: their parents had a lot of time for them. The kids were numero uno, particularly in the last years of the marriage and in the initial period of separation. So no matter who you are, coming into this family, you will generally be received with resentment, either outright or hidden. The key to step-parenting is to not take that resentment personally. Because it is not personal, it happens in all blended families.

The most important step you can take is acknowledging how tough it is, and how tough it is going to be for everyone.

Denim and I walked into our relationship assuming it was going to be easy. Our kids loved each other and we have similar ideals and values, etc. We were so optimistic. But we've had our problems; my kids drive him crazy a lot of the time. While I'm kind of immune to the sound of yelling and punching and throwing things at each other, it really agitates Denim. I often think if we had acknowledged how hard it was going to be, we would be less hard on ourselves now when things get tough.

Honestly? The key to life is lowering our expectations. Bring down the standards, bring down the expectations. If I told you that step-parenting is the hardest thing in the world and most people end up in a stress coma, you'd think you were winning coz all you feel is resentment over someone eating your last fucking Golden Gaytime.

But if I were to tell you that step-parenting is a breeze, it's a blessing, hashtag blessed, hashtag family, hashtag fuck off? You'd think you had failed miserably and need another 48 Golden Gaytimes to stuff down your resentful throat. Lower the expectations. This is a tough gig with teething problems that can last years.

Now that you have taken authority away from your relationship with the kids, think about all the fun that you can have, the friendship. You can be the person the kids go to when their parent is just too intense. You can be the important person to this child, just by being there.

My stepdad came into my life when I was eleven. Never once has he yelled at me, disciplined me or been disappointed in me, and do you know why? Because he literally has no ego and there is no room for an ego when step-parenting. You just have to cop it on the chin.

And do you know what? He separated from my mum five years ago and has lived with me on and off ever since, with my kids who adore their grandad and my partner who loves him. He will be the first to tell you that step-parenting a brat paid off in the long run, with one of the most fulfilling long-term relationships I've ever, ever been in.

One day, just after getting snapped at to get out of the kitchen and stop picking at my cooking, Billie-Violet asked me why I didn't yell at Zeyke when he did the same thing twenty minutes later. I had to think about it for a minute, because I didn't want her to resent him, and I didn't want to be unfair. I explained to her, "You know I love you. I have kissed you every day for over eight years. I can snap at you, and you giggle. Zeyke doesn't have that privilege yet; he doesn't know how much I love him. So, until he does, I'll let him eat a mashed potato before the meat is ready."

It's really hard and can take years to get right. God knows Denim and I still have a long way to go (and by that, I mean Denim still has a long way to go. I clearly get it!).

But when I interviewed the amazing Steve Biddulph (from *Raising Boys* and *Manhood*) and I asked him all about step-parenting and told him I was finding the whole gig complicated, he responded, "Well, just remind your children that they have parents who love them; they have to love them, it's their jobs. Step-parents don't have to be there, they don't have to love them. They choose to, they made a choice to stick around and love this whole family."

How much of a bonus is that?

Support Each Other

After speaking to Dr Michael Carr-Gregg, a renowned psychologist and writer of the books *Princess Bitchface Syndrome*, *Prince Boofhead Syndrome* and *Surviving Step-Families*, on the topic of clear advice for blending a family, I walked away with a healthy understanding of my road ahead.

Don't fall for the Brady Bunch illusion, where the whole family gets on, the kids are perfect, parents are in love and there is this bloody woman around that cooks and cleans for everyone, and probably blows off Mr Brady just to add to the perfection. Real life isn't like that.

He also agrees that discipline is not the job of the step-parent; building connections as friends and another positive role model is pretty much as good as it's going to get.

On a sadder note, not all step-parents are going to have a good relationship with their stepkids, and Dr Michael has told me that this is something that some people need to accept; sometimes pleasant is as good as it gets.

And it's not always the children; some step-parents just can't deal with the kids. Dr Michael spoke to me about some step-parents that just couldn't bear to be touched by their stepchildren and that just broke my heart. How could children be raised in an environment where an adult is cringing at the thought of them snuggling up to them on the couch?

But really, a huge role for a step-parent, a role so important that it could possibly shape the child's entire life, is that of a role model in a loving relationship. Children from broken relationships more often than not haven't seen mum or dad being completely supported or loved. This relationship is the one that will need to repair the child's inner voice of what love looks like, show the child how you can support and love their parent. You could be the person in their life who sets foundations of what to expect from their very own relationships.

To recap

Those three small changes changed everything in my household. Before we made them, things didn't feel natural, new love didn't feel like new love with resentment that resembled an ancient relationship.

And I can't help myself; I resent another adult disciplining my child. I don't believe in it on the playground – I wouldn't yell at a child who threw sand at my kid, I'd talk to their folks – so why would things be any different at home?

I started looking at Denim's children differently because he was acting as if they were perfect while mine were animals, so of course, as the lioness mother, I started seeing negative behaviours in his children as a way of defending my own. That in turn didn't feel right, because I love his children so much. So he needed to back off.

I'm lucky that Denim is a quick learner and not too proud to take direction when it comes from the experts, and the family has never been happier. There are times he needs to be with his children and I still need to be with mine; we can't just pretend we were always one big family. My children still have their life outside of us, and his have a huge past that doesn't include us. But we are happy, and this is us.

So to conclude:

Don't try and be a disciplinary figure – that is not the job of a step-parent.

Lower your expectations and stop kidding yourself. This is hard; it requires a lot of work and will take time for your own unique family groove to set in.

Support each other and be the loving connection that these children need to witness.

And don't give up, because a big, beautiful, colourful, splendid family of children who have learnt how to love, how to invite new people into the home and how to love people who aren't blood-related is the most rewarding thing you can ask for.

For more information Dr Michael Carr-Gregg's book *Surviving Step-Families* is available on Amazon and is a must-read.

Lower your expectations.

Step-parenting is extremely hard. Stop lying to yourself and pretending "We will be the perfect blended family, I will love his like my own and vice versa". NO. It's hard.

Stop trying to discipline each other's children. You are not their parent. You could be a fantastic parent figure or friend, or you could be the biggest enemy, troll, arsehole.

You don't have to love each other but you have to co-exist harmoniously. Love is a bonus, step-parents can also be a bonus, but the pressure needs to come off.

Be a team with your lover. Nobody needs time alone, have date nights and take special care of each other, like the parents of a blended family. You guys made the brave decision to climb the steep hill of dealing with exes and blending kids. You deserve the very best of each other.

UP THE BLOODY DUFF, AGAIN

Welcome to Mumming.

You are going to love it.

Just a couple of things...

You'll start work at 5.30am and finish at... hang on, we'll come back to this one.

You definitely get a lunch break; most of us like to take roughly three seconds to stuff kids' leftovers into our mouths on their way to the bin. Great for the waistline... well...

Holidays? Of course you get holidays. Only you must work harder than usual; kids leave their routines at home, partners need to relax and "unwind" after all the hard work they did to pay for this trip. Have fun!!!

We believe health is the foundation of all good parenting, so if you are sick, please take the time and consideration to pretend you're not. And continue holding the house together, for the greater health... of your family.

Mental health. We've found that a lot of new mums find this twenty-year commitment daunting. We struggle to understand why, but if you do need some assistance in the mental health sector you are welcome to take it... just don't tell anyone... we may have to resort to labelling you as someone who didn't take to mumming naturally, which may lead to the label "not coping" which could then lead to the label "lost the plot".

Your performance will be rated by the one thing you have little control over – your baby, child and partner's behaviour in public.

Overtime? We don't like our mums to call it overtime, we like them to call it "family time"; the time the family gets to present you with complaints while you are trying to shit or sleep or pay a bill on the internet.

Don't forget your new uniform. This ripped-up top with spaghetti marks, that you are pretty sure you mopped piss with last week, and a pair of baggy stained undies with pubes sticking out of them.

Oh, and one more thing: just prepare yourself for a bunch of royal fuckwits to ask you what you do all day.

Enjoy!!!

And don't forget to be, above all else... #blessed.

If you have any further queries, don't bother complaining. We will only label you ungrateful.

Con xx

The most important thing about pregnancy is "me time". Time to rejoice in the amazing journey that your body is going through and become at one with the experience, breathe in… and out.

OK, truth? Cheeseburgers are the most important thing during pregnancy, and time alone to masturbate. I don't know why but orgasms are ten-fold when I'm up the duff.

Nobody has the time to rejoice in the journey; they barely have the energy to breathe. Pregnancy is kind of like a nine-month hangover, only most of the time there was no wild night.

Instead of a raucous one-night stand, you lay on your back, counting down the minutes while you're inseminated by your partner's semi-hard stiffy.

Or you're the other type, one of those odd folks who have a loving relationship and a fulfilling sex life, and the miracle of life is just as precious as the time your boyfriend gave you head while on your period. Smitten.

And, of course, all of the conceptions in between – the girl who got knocked up at a club by a stranger, the one time you fucked your ex without a condom and was more worried about the possibility of catching HIV than getting pregnant, and those that have tried and tried and tried, and the day before they gave up, a little baby was created.

Whether it was an accident or an eagerly awaited dream, most of us can relate to one thing – nine months of uncertainty. And here is a fact – it isn't even nine months, it's fucking ten! #theworldsbestkeptsecret. Which never worked in my favour because for some reason, when I'm pregnant I always round the pregnancy up; if I'm ten weeks, I say I'm eleven; if I'm fourteen weeks, I say I'm sixteen. I have no idea why I do that.

During my first ever pregnancy, I was at a gathering, talking to a woman who was also pregnant. I was 25 weeks and thought I was the first woman to ever get knocked up. I started talking to her and asked her how far along she was, assuming I was further along than her because – you know when people say, "I was the size of a house"? Well, if I was a block of apartments, she'd have been the mailbox. And she turned around and told me she was thirty weeks. I remember the distinct feeling of defeat. She had won the pregnancy competition, and I was nothing but an oversized apartment block who ate too much. If only I had rounded my pregnancy up that little bit more, I could have at least cheated my way to the finish line.

But unfortunately, my babies all came early, so while I was telling people I was nine months instead of eight and a premature baby came and we were stuck in hospital for a month and all my friends were like, "How can she be so premature when you were full term like a month ago?" Lying never pays, kids.

It's a *slow* ten months. And we all have to go through it if we want to have a baby to complain about for the next eighteen years.

The month I fell pregnant with Denim was a very weird month. I had gone off the pill because it had flared up my colitis, and in the previous few months, I had taken the morning-after pill at the slightest hint that we may have had a risky frisky encounter.

At my local chemist, there is a little room that they put you in when you ask for the morning-after pill. I think it's there for privacy but I told Denim it's my "dirty little slut room".

The second time I took the morning-after pill was in Melbourne. All of our kids were with us and we went to a really dodgy looking chemist in St Kilda. I spent a good portion of my childhood in the dodgy part of St Kilda, so I know that the pharmacists there have better things to worry about then a dirty little slut, so they don't even give you your own room.

The pharmacist did however look at my screaming kids who were pulling each other's hair, begging for cough lollies and trying to steal shit and said loudly, "I should be giving you this morning-after pill for free, or I could charge you three times the amount. God knows you need it." And the whole chemist's burst into laughter. I laughed too; he was right. Now, gimme the fucking pill!!

Eventually, when I stopped taking the pill and got my ulcerative colitis back on track, Denim and I started the withdrawal method. A method created by someone who wanted lots of kids.

I know, I know. God knows I know. But you see, doing anything permanent wasn't an option because we knew we wanted a baby after the wedding and next tour.

The thing is that Denzy is really, really good at withdrawing. You know how some men say they are going to withdraw, but they just have to give it one more thrust coz it feels so goddamn goo... "Shit, sorry!"

Well, that's not Denzy. When he is even near cumming, he literally throws me away from him; like two magnets on opposing sides, I miraculously repel to the other side of the bed and he wanks it out. I told him, "Sometimes I just feel like you're having a wank next to me, you're so careful."

So I felt good about it. One month, we had a dodgy moment where he may have not pulled out in time and my period was like four days late, which is rare for me, but I took a pregnancy test and it was negative and I got my period the next day... so relieved.

I mean, I definitely wanted a baby with Denim but just not now, when I was focused on my kids, blending this beautiful family, work... OK, and looking hot as fuck walking down the aisle, not rolling down it like a bee-stung ball of tits and tummy.

The following month, something really odd happened. We had all been sick all month. I mean really sick. When I get the flu, I suffer from terrible migraines, and Denim and I were staying at his mum's house and I was about halfway through my cycle when I got this splitting migraine. I was shaking in agony all night; no pills could cut through the pain and I asked Denim to take me to the hospital. Half-asleep, he managed to tell me that there wasn't a hospital anywhere near us, we were in the country and I just put up with the evening of agony.

The following night it was my stomach, cramping up like you wouldn't believe, period pain on steroids. I went to the toilet, shaking, and I got the beginning of my period, just a bit on the toilet paper. I thought it was strange as my period never does this kind of radical shit, maybe my period had its period? I came back to bed and told Denzy I had my period, all he can think of is, "Awesome. Period week means no withdrawing," and, confused, I went to bed.

Later that month, we were heading to Bali with my sister and cousin. My period never actually came after that night at Denim's mum's house, and my nipples were getting sore. The actual due date of my period was the day before we left for Bali and it never came. The next day, it didn't come. I kept telling Denim I thought I was pregnant, but he didn't care because I think I'm pregnant every month. I'm like the girl who cried pregnant.

And finally, my boobs were so sore that one night while we were out, I saw a chemist, googled the Indonesian word for pregnant and bought a pregnancy test. I took it into a toilet and as my cousin and Denim were waiting patiently my cousin asked Denim if he was nervous. "Nah, of course not, she does this every month. Even when she's on the pill she thinks she's pregnant."

I soon opened the door the toilet. Both sets of eager eyes on me.

"Well?"

"I fucked the test. Seriously, I pissed on the wrong bit and got an inconclusive result."

They were both furious with me. What kind of 34-year-old mother pisses on the wrong side of a pregnancy test?! I told Denim to take me home early because my phantom pregnancy was making me tired.

The next day was round two. I walked up to the chemist and bought another test, took it back to our hotel and pissed on the correct piss station.

This time I got my response: "Hamil". Meaning pregnant.

My stomach dropped. In my heart, I knew this was the answer... but I really wanted to look beautiful at my wedding and I didn't know if I had the strength for the public backlash that would happen when I announced that I was pregnant. For some reason, pregnancy announcements bring out the worst in your haters. They really can't believe that you'd have the nerve to go and get pregnant. How could you do that to them?

I walked out of the toilet.

Denim and I had previously discussed that if we fell pregnant, we would keep it; we both love babies and now the twins are three, life is getting a bit easier. We are so in love. There is not really any reason to not have the baby.

So I showed him the test, I explained what "Hamil" meant. And his supportive, loving soul mate response? "Well, that's the end of all of our fun."

And that hurt. Why? Because he was right. That was the end of our fun. I had just come out of the hardest time of my life. Twins can actually ruin you. Twins will grind you up into nothing, leaving you a pile of ash on the floor, and rebuild you exactly the way they want you.

I was just out of that and it was terrifying to think I was going back into that den. Of course we considered an abortion, I'd be lying if I said we didn't. But I just couldn't shake the feeling that I wanted to share this with him, I wanted to see his face when this baby came out into the world and squinted its eyes open for the first time. I felt like I deserved that, I deserved to do this with Denim, a man who loved and supported me every day.

So I sulked. Well, I ate for two and I sulked. I'm not good at cooking or cleaning or numbers or paying bills, but when I am pregnant, I could enter the Sulking Olympics.

And of course, Denim realised that was a dumb thing to say, but he was kind of in shock. After all, I was the girl who cried pregnant all month, and we had hardly fucked that month as we all had that bloody sickness. To this day, Denim and I can't work out when this baby was conceived.

Pregnancy isn't always a miracle. It can be a mistake and a pain in the arse. We don't consider it a miracle when the rat who's been living in our roof gets touched by the blessing of new life.

Don't let guilt take over when not wanting a pregnancy; women have died terminating pregnancies, they have dedicated their lives fighting for our rights to choose, they have suffered and lived in shame. Be proud of your rights as a woman.

It can also be the moment that defines you and changes everything and gives you reason to live. Just like everyone is different, every pregnancy is different too.

PREGNANCY: IT'S JUST SO MUCH FUN

Now that the "jizz machine" has inseminated you, you could either:

Be completely oblivious to the fact and carry on like normal for like two months before you're like, "Pretty sure I had ovaries and a period at some point in my life?"

OR

Like three minutes after you conceive, be like, "Fuck, my tits hurt. Go make me some toast, I think I'm pregnant." Just like me. (In spite my lack of meditation, I am pretty in tune with my body.)

Of course, you won't get a positive pregnancy test until your period is due and there is absolutely no point in doing one early, trust me.

The First Trimester

The first trimester is all about finding your groove: are you going to be one of those mums that obeys all the rules, ditches feta and takes up yoga? Are you going to resign from work and give it everything you've got? Or are you going to wing it, keep working, live your life to the max and give no fucks about what the books say you "should" be doing? After all, pregnancy is the most natural thing you will ever do in your life, so why not just follow your instincts, if, of course, your instincts are in check…

Some people's instincts tell them what the baby needs. For example, I always crave oranges and it turns out I'm low in iron and your body needs vitamin C to process iron properly.

However, not everyone's instincts are in check. If they are telling you to keep clubbing and that a line or two of cocaine will be fine… go get those books again, you might learn something.

The first decision that most Queens come across is, "Who will I tell?" And if you want my advice, the answer is everyone! Tell all the people all the things all the time. We like to call it oversharing, and it's healthy and glorious.

My reason why? The whole reason people are told to keep the baby to themselves when they are pregnant is in case they lose it. To avoid having awkward conversations when people ask how the baby is. We know better now. Back when these guidelines were first suggested, people still thought of a miscarriage as something to be ashamed of, as if it was in some way the fault of the mother. This is so outdated, even my conservative obstetrician told me that he recommended his wife told as many people as she wanted. Not only does this remove the stigma of miscarriage, but it also ensures a huge support network in case anything does happen. The truth is that most of my friends tell me that they're pregnant before their husbands have even come home from work to hear the good news. And guess who would be first on the scene if anything were to happen? Moi.

Now you have to get used to being bloated. I know that not everyone has this same problem as me, but once I get my period, I lose lots of weight in fluids; I can wear jeans again and rediscover my cheekbones.

So when that period is Houdini, I never get to let go of any of those fluids, and when I'm bloated, my brain changes to "well, I'm already fat" mode and I eat. Cheat meal, cheat life.

It's really quite depressing looking 163 months pregnant at six weeks. No matter how many times you promise yourself that this time, you'll be controlled like the celebrities, and give in to no cravings. Then your doctor is "gonna wanna" do all the tests, like the ones you've been putting off for years. Ya know, the old clap test, blood counts (not fun for cancer-phobes like me) and of course, everyone's favourite, HIV.

I don't care how much of a saint you've been, or how many randoms that look like they have drug problems you "didn't fuck" in a car outside a nightclub. Nobody wants to get an HIV test.

I have HIV paranoia. I believe it is a mild form of post-traumatic stress left over from being a tiny little girl and watching the "Grim Reaper" ads from the 80s. I used to have nightmares about it: the one where the Grim Reaper has a bowling ball and he's striking down all the trapped people, kids and women holding babies. I used to watch it, paralysed, and dream that when I fell asleep, my mum and sister turned into Grim Reapers. So naturally, I have always thought I had AIDS.

And then they want to weigh you.

Now, for every other pregnancy, I have let them weigh me and have ended up devastated at my weight, despite the majority of it being fluid and tits… and chocolate and McFlurrys… and I am left miserable. One pregnancy, I became so miserable that I tried to starve myself and actually considered resuming my bulimia days. When that didn't work, the depression kicked in. Crying-myself-to-sleep depression.

The funny misconception with pregnancy is that all of your eating and body image issues will just fly away because this is your "time off" but that is certainly not the case. In fact, for many women, it just gets worse.

Learning to overcome eating and body image disorders has a lot to do with knowing and avoiding triggers. Scales can be a huge trigger for me, so when the doctors try to weigh me, I try and refuse, but they always insist, and I end up having to face the other way.

So many nurses have laughed at me. Once when I stood on the scales backwards, one said patronisingly to her colleague, "We have eating disorders over here," and they both chuckled.

And do you know what? I couldn't give a fuck. It is better than hating yourself for a number on the scales that you cannot change and not being able to sleep.

And then you get your blood-test results, and just like that you are so glad that you sat through them, that you didn't chicken out and refuse to have them. Nothing feels better than knowing that you didn't catch AIDS that time you stepped on something sharp at the beach, and even your walk changes into that walk that you can only do with a syphilis-free fanny in between your legs. Yeah, baby.

The Second Trimester

The second trimester is the fun part. You've gone from a slightly green colour and spewing in public bins with no belly at all, which makes everyone think you just mixed up slightly too much smack with your morning hit, to a glowing pregnant woman with a beautiful belly.

Only, not a whole lot more happens. Yeah, you have the odd gestational diabetes test that you will convince yourself you have, as all you eat is chocolate and cake. But one thing you will know for sure, and you may or may not be right, is that fasting for the blood test will make you realise how much of your time is taken up by either eating, or planning to eat.

And then there will be a few emotional breakdowns. You know, the standard stuff: *fuck everyone I'm finding a rental and setting up fetish cams, coz none of you cunts understand me.*

A doctor will hand you a really long cottonwool bud and ask you to violate your arsehole with it, masking the assault with the words "anal swab". Be sure to really clean the old haemorrhoids before doing that, we all know the swabs are more for the judgement of the doctor than they are about your baby's health.

Which will bring you to the final trimester.

The Third Trimester

This is pretty much just full of sound effects: complaining, farting without warning, and literally discarding everything you drop – unless it's your only saviour, your phone – in which case, you can cue the sound effects again. Constantly thinking you are in labour, tossing and turning for thirty minutes until you are finally comfortable and then realising you need to piss.

I like to refer to this stage as "given up". It is the pregnancy equivalent of that time I gained heaps of weight and then cut off my hair because I was tired of pretending to myself that I was remotely hot.

The nice maternity clothes turn into a rotation of Kmart nighties, and Ugg boots are the only shoes that will accommodate your swollen feet. Kindly replying to the polite questions that strangers ask with "33 weeks" has turned into a blank stare and an accidental-on-purpose burp.

And you start to wonder: will I ever feel energetic again? The fear and anxiety over the impending lack of sleep ironically gives you sleepless nights. You hate everyone and the most confusing part is that the one thing you've been dreading your whole life – childbirth – you now can't wait for. That's the miracle of pregnancy; it's so fucked that it can actually make you look forward to childbirth.

But wait… there's more. Forums. All the forums you could ask for. Because you can't be fucked moving and don't have the patience for talking, so every thought that pops into your mind is typed out in Google, which leads to a forum with a bunch of other anti-social mums who want to know the same things.

I remember googling: *How do I know if my body is getting ready for labour?* Hoping to God that I would click onto something that would say: *You, Constance, are in labour.*

I will never forget what I once stumbled across with my relentless googling:

I knew I was in soon to be in labour because my husband is a farmer, and he was in the bathroom with me while I was showering, and when I bent over to grab something he said that my vagina was all puffed up like the cows in our paddocks look just before they begin to labour.

Hmm. A really bizarre and intriguing comment, cue mirror grab. Now, I had not seen my vagina in quite some time and I have no idea what a cow's fanny looks like even before labour and, to be honest, I'd be too scared to google such a thing in case there is a room in my local police station that would sound an alarm with my address and police would arrive accusing me of bestiality. So I'm just going to imagine that one. But I'm not going to say it looked like a delightful little butterfly wing; it had a definite puff to it, and it wasn't a pretty little smooth porn puss.

If you're a savvy internetter, you could even find forums where women overshare photos of their experiences: their puffy fannies, their mucus plugs, the lot. In fact, when you finally do give birth, you'll need a bit of a "soul cleaning" over all the things you looked up in your final trimester – porn, birth forums – it's a pretty strange couple of months.

Hint: It's not much fun.

The first trimester sucks because you don't look pregnant so nobody treats you like the procreating goddess you deserve to be treated like.

The second trimester sucks because you feel good but still can't drink.

The third trimester sucks because finally you're being treated like the sexual and fertile goddess of life, but you can't enjoy it because your hormones have you convinced that you are surrounded by a bunch of cunts.

The perfect childbirth is the one where you come out of it happy and proud of yourself. Be proud that you created a baby, one that was pulled out by forceps, or yanked out of your tummy or pushed out in a blow-up pool. Be proud: you are a wild, wicked woman.

WHAT TO EXPECT WHEN YOU'RE EXPECTING EVERYTHING TO BE OK: PERINATAL DEPRESSION AND ANXIETY

Truthfully, I do think pregnancy is funny. Being constantly weighed, tested for hepatitis, anally swabbed, asked about abortion history, vaginally probed, telling your doctor the colour and smell of your discharge, all leading towards the day that you're gonna shit into your doctor's or husband's hands, before a tiny pink baby squeezes out, stretching your vagina so much that you'll laugh out a tampon for the rest of your life.

If you didn't laugh, you'd cry. Or, like me, you can do both.

I laugh about how fucked pregnancy is because I want to lower everyone's expectations of it. If all we know of pregnancy are the professional maternity photo shoots we constantly see on our newsfeeds, and we compare them to ourselves lying on the lounge room floor, crying because we can't reach the remote control, and googling to see if our husband is a sociopath because he went to work even though you told him that he had to stay home today because your fanny looks like a cow's fanny and you think you're going into labour, then you will become really depressed. You could easily slip into:

"What's wrong with me? Why am I so down while everyone else is enjoying this?"

When I'm pregnant, I worry about so much: the baby's health, my weight, the birth. Will I bleed out? Is my iron too low? What if something happens during the caesarean? Pre-eclampsia can kill you? *What the fuck?*

All these things can stress you out so much, while we neglect the one thing that we actually need to be alarmed by. The number one killer in pregnancy is suicide.

Unmanaged perinatal depression and anxiety is the most dangerous thing you will come across from the time that you conceive. Forget the scary blood tests and uncomfortable examinations, and worry about your mind. Put your energy into your mind.

I should know, I suffer from severe perinatal anxiety. I can't sleep, I can't stop worrying about things that I have known my whole life, but now make everything feel like doomsday. That's what anxiety is; it's an impending doom.

This pregnancy is so strange. My partner loves and supports me. I am independent, nobody can kick me out of the house that I own, I am in a better place than I have been my whole life, yet still I live with butterflies in my tummy.

When a friend messages me: *Can we talk?* I freak out and call and call and call, until I get through, panicked over not knowing what they are going to say. And they are all: "Can you wear purple and orange together?"

Anxiety makes me freak out over everything, and when there is nothing to freak out over, I'll freak out over nothing. But the defining difference for me? I have some help. I know what I have, I know it's an illness, and I demand that everyone

285

treats me in the way that they would treat me if I had a physical illness – help me, do not stress me out, forgive me when I seem like a paranoid nutcase. Accept and support me. I tell people the moment I meet them.

I missed a call from an unrecognised number yesterday and listened to the voicemail, called the number back and said, "Hi, it's Constance. I didn't answer your call because I suffer from anxiety and it doesn't let me answer numbers that I don't know." The guy from the hair extension company was confused as fuck.

I don't care; I'm removing the stigma. I also know that only highly intelligent and empathetic people suffer from anxiety, so I'm cool with it getting around.

Anxiety doesn't survive in the light. The more that you talk about it, the more you expose it, the further away it goes, the weaker a grip it has on you. I have interviewed women who have wanted to commit suicide out of the blue, four days after giving birth, and met women who wanted to kill themselves and their babies during perinatal depression. This is scary shit.

I have met thousands of women from all over the world with perinatal anxiety and depression, and do you know what the common denominator was? The reason they were at my shows with a glowing smile, a friend and a glass of champers? They all courageously got help. A chemical imbalance was plaguing them, and they could not save themselves on their own.

Now, I used to think that support groups were full of old women who would judge me, like the child health nurse did the day that I broke down into tears in front of her out of sheer exhaustion. But I have recently interviewed so many women who work for various organisations who support women going through this, and they are nothing like it.

Do you know what they are? Queens. Like you and like me, the majority of the women I meet whose job it is to help you are only in those positions because they have been there. They tell their stories before they talk to me, and the stories of all the brave women that they help.

Sometimes we need an empathetic ear, like having a wine with an old friend. I feel the need to blurt my problems out to these women and it's so healing. Sometimes we need medication, and that is OK too.

If you have ever listened to anything that I have ever said (and some of it is shit, I'll own that) but this I do know: Don't be afraid to make that call.

If you are down, crying, feeling isolated, overwhelmed, there is no problem too small or too big to share with these experienced women, and who knows? Maybe this is part of your journey. To overcome something this tough and move on to becoming another Queen who's going to pull Queens out of the darkness, with your own experiences and empathy.

Pregnancy can be an amazing experience of bliss and connection, or it can suck on a bag of steaming dicks. Hang in there. Your path is unique, it's only for you and everything is temporary.

To: All of my Queens who have, or are about to have, a baby.

I get a lot of messages from miserable Queens after having babies.

It's not easy to be in a depressing situation without getting depression.

So together I think we need to make parenthood less depressing.

Having had four babies, two psychologists, one marriage counsellor, severe anxiety, four break ups and make ups... I am in the position to offer this advice:

Socialise. Please.

Above cleaning, above cooking, above everything.

Because face-to-face contact is free therapy; a laugh and a coffee or walk saved me, even on days that I did not want to I followed my psychologist's advice and forced myself to.

Placing a new 24-hour job between two parents is going to cause friction, it just is. When we get stressed, we blame each other.

But the working parent is able to walk out the door and distract themselves, kick goals at work, have a chat and just generally feel like a normal human with a purpose, whereas the at-home parent is home, left to dwell on the argument and maximise everything that was said, so by the time the worker comes home he is normal, and wifey is a crazed lunatic who has packed her bags and is selling the house.

That's not fair. It's not fair that we get the word "depression" thrown at us when we don't have the opportunity to heal in these four walls.

You deserve a life despite becoming a mum.

You have two huge responsibilities: keeping your baby safe and happy, and taking care of your mental health. Everything else can wait.

If anyone questions that, explain that socialising is your mental health plan. We all need a mental health plan, parenthood should come with one.

Walk out that door and call a Queen, even if you barely know her. Talk openly, bitch about the dickhead you married, cry about your lack of sleep, laugh at the state of the house you just walked out of. Just do it. Stop cancelling on your friends; cancel everything else, not friends. You will feel healed. You might even love your partner more.

Remember Queens: parenthood's most vital tool is your happiness.

Con x

If you are, or anyone you know is, in crisis or experiencing suicidal thoughts, please reach out for help:

Australia
Lifeline: 13 11 14 or www.lifeline.org.au
Panda (Perinatal Anxiety & Depression Australia):
1300 726 306 or www.panda.org.au
Beyond Blue: 1300 22 4636 or www.beyondblue.org.au

UK
www.pandasfoundation.org.uk

USA
www.postpartum.net
Or if you go to: www.postpartumprogress.com

There is a comprehensive list of helplines and website supports groups in Australia, Canada, Ireland, Scotland, New Zealand, South Africa, the UK and the USA.

Only the cleverest, kindest and prettiest women suffer from anxiety or depression.

Perinatal anxiety affects so many of us, that there is no reason why it shouldn't be spoken about like any other aspect of parenthood, "How's the reflux? Is he sleeping? How's your depression going?"

Use the services. JUST USE THE SERVICES. And you know what else? Use the fucking services.

LOVE CONQUERED

TOURING THE WORLD, LOVING MY MAN AND ALL THE SHIT THAT COMES WITH WOMEN WHO SUCCEED

Denzy and I had only been together for a few weeks, days, minutes, when we knew that this was it, that we were it for each other.

I had never had great luck with blokes, they always thought I was too much, too loud. Breaking into their house at 3am dressed up as a fat Catwoman wasn't cute, it was creepy. Or some unappreciative shit like that. Men have never really understood my romantic ways.

Denzy, on the other hand, I make sense to. Everything I did worked for him. I would look at him and think, "This is your cue to run."

And he'd turn to me and say, "That is why I love you."

Not that many men fit in with my chaos, but Denim's chilled nature was just perfect; he just never minds about anything. We often speak about how everything in our whole lives had just been training for the day that we met.

Still, I felt unsure for so long, unsure that he wouldn't up and leave me. I have massive abandonment issues; if a guy takes too long to shit, I feel abandoned. If he offers to go and pick up dinner? Abandoned.

So Denzy was in the unique position of convincing this tortured little creep that he wasn't going anywhere. And bit by bit, it was working.

The things that would freak most men out, like how many kids I have, or the fact that I blog about the explicit details of my life to over a million women, just made him love me more. And the things that would freak most women out, like Denim's drug history or the fact that he didn't work, just made me understand and love him more.

I needed someone to be with me. I'd felt alone my whole life, and the fact that Denim had made the decision to just be with his kids and go without the creature comforts of the world was all I wanted.

Despite being financially independent, I don't need expensive things. My jewellery would be considered costume jewellery to most people, and just today a guy I work with at the radio station confessed that the first time he saw me in a studio, he told a colleague that a homeless chick had snuck in and was sleeping in Studio 9.

If I had a dollar for every time I was questioned over the fact that Denim doesn't work, I'd be able to retire. Leaving work to travel with his children was the best decision Denim ever made. When I met him, he was about to start working again. Then he travelled with me, and now between our six kids and one on the way, and my ridiculously busy lifestyle, it makes no sense at all for Denim to work. I need him too much.

We survive on the weekly money my company pays me, and we run out of money before every payday. If I didn't work and looked after the kids, everyone would be happy because a woman should sacrifice her career to motherhood. A man doing the same thing just doesn't suit a lot of people's idea of a family.

Some people can't stand to see the freedom I have to pursue my career. Why? Because it's not fair that I'm able to have all these kids, as well as a man who's prepared to sacrifice all his time to support my dreams.

The more I got to know Denzy, the more I realised that his upbringing was pretty normal. His parents are still together. His mum will stand up for him no matter what, and his dad is really knowledgeable and Denim quotes him all the time. In fact, had Denzy not gone down the path that he went down with drugs and addiction, he might have been a little too privileged for my taste.

I always end up getting rid of blokes who haven't been through anything, because I have been through so much in my life and I don't like being judged or misunderstood by someone whose life has been a white picket fence, and whose toughest decisions were based around being too hungry for a six-inch, but not hungry enough for a foot-long.

My childhood was far from normal. At my 21st, my dad told the story that I rolled my first spliff aged two. I chopped up some grass and, full of pride, wrapped it in a paper and handed it to him. Ironically, I don't smoke cigarettes and have never smoked pot.

My mum's favourite stories of me are always the ones of me singing and dancing on the stage at our local pubs while her boyfriend played in the band. I have nothing against a conventional upbringing; I just know that non-conventional ones work too. The world is full of so many colourful people, why give everyone the same childhood?

I need understanding and empathy. The biggest turn-on a guy can do for me is never be grossed out. You know, guys who don't let chicks wee in front of them and won't fuck you on your period? I cannot deal with that shit. I need a man who ignores the fart that smells like a rotting baby lamb, one who laughs when he pulls his dick out on period week and it looks like an extra from *The Texas Chainsaw Massacre*.

I remember the first time I vomited in front of Denim. He was lying in bed and I ran to the toilet to spew, more than a bit of wee was forced out as I dry-retched and burped at the same time. Heaving sounds, farts and bile – it was a sight. Denzy offered to help but I shooed him away.

When I finally made it back to bed, I asked him if it was a huge turn-off and he responded, "You could spew on my face and it wouldn't turn me off." Then he kissed my stinky lips and went back to sleep. #soulmates.

I soon realised that if anything had played out differently, we wouldn't have ended up here together. Everything we had gone through was all building up to the moment that we met. Within days of meeting, we spoke about what we would name a baby if we had one. Within weeks, we joked about getting married; within a month of getting together, we decided to tattoo each other's names on our arms; and within two months, Denzy had proposed to me. Only neither of us can actually remember it.

More on that in a bit.

We were on tour in England, Ireland and Scotland, which couldn't have come at a better time. I had to get out of the country because… well, everyone here hated me. It felt like Australia had turned on me and for some reason, other countries couldn't give a fuck about my life fuck-ups; they were forgiving and loyal, while Australia was looking for any excuse to rip shreds off me.

Honestly, looking back, while it felt like everyone in Australia hated me, the truth is that my loyal followers didn't go anywhere. The haters had become louder. My loyal followers sat back and stuck around; nobody follows me because they want someone to hate on, they follow me because they are sick of the hate and want to just hear some love.

In fact, at one point someone said to me, "Anyone who leaves you now, who joins your hate groups, who bitches about you online now, was never a Queen anyway, was never part of your incredible community."

And the best thing they said to me?

"Even if your following dwindled down to three, three Queens who had your back and supported you in any decision, you'd be OK. You'd go back to cutting again and sweeping floors for a living, but you'd still be OK."

All I did on tour was work. PR interviews, live shows and travelling. While everyone else on tour gets days off, if I had one, some PR would be squeezed into it. The whole thing was just so bizarre. It's one thing to get attention online, but, like the hate, you learn to take the love with a grain of salt too.

Part of me was proud of myself. Taking this guy on tour helped me see with fresh eyes what had happened to my life. All of my shows had sold out and I had to put on extra ones; a guy from a newspaper, who had just photographed Prince Harry, photographed me; I was recognised on the streets of London and asked for pictures. It was such a strange feeling, and whenever I had any time to myself to reflect, I just couldn't believe it was me; that this had happened to *me*.

In Belfast, women were bursting into tears when they saw me; women in Leeds were staying back after the show to give me presents and ended up partying with my crew; women told me that they had wanted to commit suicide until they found us, the Queens, supporting each other through real shit, not the superficial crap that you find on the internet.

I think about these women, I let their faces sink into my mind and I sit back but I can't pinpoint the feeling – is it pride? Am I proud to have started this community that saves women's lives through connection?

No, it's honoured. I haven't done anything to be proud of, I'm just so honoured that so many people tune into me, hear my fuck-ups, tell me (and the whole community) their own, and celebrate each other through the connection we all share.

Denim could not believe it either. I remember him telling me one day that he had no idea what a big deal I was. I guess my life is pretty low-key. I'm run off my feet with my four kids. I have managers and a CEO and a company spread out in Melbourne and Perth, but they really keep the business side of things away from me.

When you make the decision to do everything yourself, publish and distribute your own book, not align with any companies, never advertise on your page, and create your own clothing line, you need strong management behind you, which I have. My only request from them is that I'm not burdened with the details of anything. I'm a creative; one phone call from an accountant will confuse and freak me out so much that I won't be able to write for a week.

So my stresses are limited to whether I can squeeze in a Woolworths shop before picking up the twins, or whether I have to pick the twins up and spend an extra $400 on everything they see in every fucking aisle.

I have never felt like a big deal. I feel like a fraud most days. I'm not a master of anything, I'm not an expert, I'm a person who, for whatever reason, a lot of people love and a lot of people hate.

Your real friends will want to see you happy, want to see you succeed.

Misery loves company. When someone chooses to judge you, or can't be around you now that you have decided to become happy, you are simply confronting their unhappiness, which hurts. They may well choose to stay around people who help them ignore it. And that's OK – everyone is on their own path.

Never give up on true love, no matter who you are, how old you are, how many kids you have or how unworthy you feel. You're worthy.

DENZY PROPOSED AND FIXED THE UNFIXABLE

When the tour was over, I got smashed. The kids were with their nannies, who came on tour with me so I didn't drown in parental guilt, and I went out with the team. I drank and drank and danced on tables. I made my sister drink, who then basically spent her whole night worrying about me. I started fights with Denzy, begged him to forgive me, told everyone how much I loved them, got kicked out of a bar, came home and went down for a long, long dry-mouthed sleep.

This could have been the night that Denim proposed. We don't know. All we know is that we were holidaying in southern Italy after our tour and we were in Positano, in a restaurant called Penguins, with the kids, my sister and her kids. Denim was festively tipsy when he got down on one knee. He told me that it is clear our souls were destined to be together and he would be honoured to be my husband.

My sister looked at me shocked. I turned to her and said, "Don't worry, he's already proposed to me and I've already said yes, only neither of us know when or where. We both just know that it had happened."

My sister's eyes calmed, almost as if she didn't need to

congratulate us because we were only fucking around. I said yes. Again. And we continued on with our fairytale romance.

Denim and I knew that we weren't fucking around. We had had so many moments of deep connection, he had told me that before he met me, he knew that if anything ever happened to his kids, he wouldn't be able to cope and he would have just given up. But now he said that I gave him something to live for, something that made him more "him" and not just as a dad.

Denim relaxed me; he hums to a very mellow tune. He doesn't let "what ifs" get to him. Denzy taught me that, for most of my life, I have been controlled by my anxiety. So many people have given me worst-case scenarios to scare me into taking their advice and doing what they wanted. These people had also been maximising drama and keeping me constantly on edge.

Denim, being the opposite, is constantly telling me, "That's not true," and "That doesn't matter," or "We will deal with that if it arises," and as a result, my anxiety levels have reduced dramatically. Even my health has improved. I have a worried mind; I hyper-focus on projects and take flyaway comments so personally. That side of Denim does not exist; he doesn't have an anxious or paranoid bone in his body.

While flying from one country to the next, we both started to miss our country, Australia. The kids were restless; they struggled in hotels and airports and wanted an Australian adventure, one without the rules around the airports and the shushing around hotels. They needed the beach, the sun, the desert.

Returning to WA was going to be a few weeks short of the end of the school term and I made the decision that I wouldn't put them straight back to school but instead, I'd give them the rest of the term off. I'd take them up the coast in WA, where the desert meets the sea, to camp and snorkel one of the best reefs in the world.

It was so beautiful. The kids came to life with the wildlife and the bonfires; it was exactly what we needed. Heaps of kids live there, and many are home-schooled, so there were children everywhere. It also has a popular surf break, so Denzy was happy too.

One evening as the sun was setting and the kids were all playing with the local kids, Denim and I went down to the ocean to put our feet in the water. The water is much warmer there coz we were further north than where we live. It is bright blue and the tall orange rocks contrast perfectly. As I soaked in the surroundings and watched the sunset, I turned around to talk to Denim I saw he was on one knee, shorts and thongs in the water.

I said, "Again?"

And he said, "Again. Properly this time. Constance Hall, as you know our love has existed before the beginning of time, please will you marry me so our souls can be entwined till the end of time."

"Yes, of course, yes."

I jumped on him, wrapping my stumpy little body around his lean muscly one and he fell, crumbling under the pressure and we both, fully clothed, got swallowed up by the foam of a broken wave.

Denim got up quickly and pulled me up, worried about my lack of abilities around all things nature and movement, but I didn't mind.

I was at peace. Denim brings me peace.

I've been restless for so long, alone in my thoughts. My dad died when I was 28 and I never recovered. Watching him die killed a piece of me, but as a mother I had no choice but to move on, to pretend that I was still me despite losing the only man who had ever understood me, been proud of me and celebrated me for just being me.

My dad used to smile at my clothes, even when I went through my 80s Madonna phase, cut-off gloves phase, huge elaborate dresses phase. My dad always said that I dressed with expression, and he was always proud of my stories. He told me that everyone who met me was lucky. He would explain stories with character voices to help my unusual brain digest the information he was trying to teach me. My dad was an artist in every sense of the word, and he knew that life wasn't going to be easy for his little quirk, but he made it simple.

And then he left me. He left us, my sister, my aunties; everyone loved him because he was made of love.

My dad used to visit me in my dreams. I'd hear his crazy laugh and run to find him, behind trees, crouching under chairs and he'd motion for me to shush and we'd hide from everyone else while he laughed. Or he'd tell me a joke, or I'd just hear him talking to someone else. Whatever it was I'd wake up so grateful that I'd heard his voice again.

And then it stopped. I assume my subconscious could no longer form his voice for me, like it was forgetting him. Or maybe he'd moved on, was being reborn, or thought I didn't need him anymore.

And then I met Denim and my heart was filled with that same peace. I shone as I heard him talk about me with pride. I felt like I was healing from internal injuries I'd become so used to, I no longer recognised them as pain.

My seventh great-grandfather's name was Michael Dwyer; he was a leader in the Irish Rebellion, a local, and certainly a family hero. My dad was obsessed with stories about him, he'd act out tales of Michael over and over again.

Dad spent time in Ireland, painting Irish pub scenes and getting to know the locals. He always wanted to go back, wanted to bring my sister and me. Even when he was incredibly sick, he told me he was buying a motorbike and travelling Ireland again.

Of course, that never happened. But I always kept some of his ashes, knowing that one day I'd take him back to Ireland.

When we arrived there on tour, my sister and I decided that the grounds of Vinegar Hill were the best place to spread Dad's ashes – a famous battle took place there, one that Michael Dwyer fought in.

We all got out of the car, freezing cold, toddlers all rugged up, a bottle of red wine and plastic cups, and we walked up to the top of the hill. We told Dad how much we loved him and threw his ashes into the air. It was a windy evening so we closed our eyes as some flew away, some flew back on us and we all just laughed and missed Dad and thought about how fucking proud he'd be of us right now.

It wasn't until we got back in the car that Denim confessed to me:

"A big chunk of your Dad's ashes landed in my wine. Hope you don't mind but I drank it. I feel Gerard, everything that you tell me about him, and I couldn't think of a better way to honour him."

Of course I didn't mind. It was weird but we are talking about a man who dug up his dead dog years after he died so he could travel Australia with the skeleton of his paw.

Over the last year, I have learnt why Dad doesn't come to my dreams anymore; he knows now that I'm OK, he's still here but he doesn't need to let me hear his laugh or feel his hands. I have my soul mate and my soul is looked after every day. My hair is stroked and forehead kissed when he thinks that I'm asleep, my Netflix is turned off when I fall asleep, my reading glasses are pulled off my face, cleaned and put back on my face. And I'm never alone. Maybe Denzy did drink a bit of my dad's soul that night.

All I know is that Dad doesn't need to worry about his little girl anymore.

Denim and I aren't perfect; he's lazy and sleeps too much and ignores me when I'm trying to gossip, but we rarely fight. We look after each other and we love each other and our children with more passion than I ever believed possible.

I thought my job in this world was kids; loving them, being loved by them. I never thought I deserved or would find Denim. But I did, and I'll be grateful and love him until we die.

And I even still want to fuck his brains out whenever I look at him.

All we have are moments. Yesterday and tomorrow don't exist. Spend your life with people that make your moments shine.

IT'S NOT THE END, THIS IS JUST THE BEGINNING

WORDS FROM DENIM'S HEART

When I first met Con, falling in love was the last thing on my mind.

The lonely years had worn me down and I had lost all hope of romantic love. Admitting defeat, I dedicated my life to my two beautiful boys and found some form of contentment. I had not completely closed my heart, but it made me feel better to stop searching and inevitably ending up feeling rejected.

A few years earlier I had given away most of my worldly possessions and was now unemployed and living in share accommodation. Ever since arriving home from our trip around Oz, I had been crippled by anxiety, depression, suicidal thoughts and low self-esteem.

I was trying really hard to put my life back together. I had been through some massive upheavals and had finally overcome my lifelong drug addiction. I really felt like I deserved things to be turning around. Unfortunately, life isn't like that. After a life of reckless drug abuse I was struggling to overcome Hep C and still carried a somewhat half-melted candle for my sadly departed ex-wife. I was paying for all those years I wasted, numbed to the world, and I was being punished for not making my health a priority. Sometimes life has to hold you down for you to truly learn a life lesson.

I had recently started a new medication to eradicate the nasty virus from my system, and had just started to emerge from the fog it had created. My boys were now lost to school, and although I never regretted it I had lost myself in the process of dedicating my life to them. To be honest I had lost faith in a large part of society but still stayed open in the hope of meeting someone genuine.

I recognised Con immediately and approached her without hesitation. There is a confidence I find with women when I don't have an ulterior motive, and Con and I gelled straight away. I already knew loads about her so I let her pry inside my mind. She was everything, and more, that I could have wished for, and was equally open to discussing her life.

The more time I spent with Con, the easier it became. It was effortless for us to spend time together and I never wanted to leave her warmth and understanding. Con is someone who asks a question and actually positively listens, without ever passing judgment. She helped restore both my self-confidence and my confidence in humanity. She was the positive influence I had been searching for, possibly for my whole life.

It's true that Con made advances to me first, but only because I'm an idiot.

I thought she was absolutely stunning from the get go but totally out of my league. What I didn't know is that Con needed me as much as I needed her.

I call Con my "Gypsy Cleopatra", and it feels like our lives have crossed before. She taught me to love again and taught me a depth to love I have never felt before… from laughing in a cafe at each other's jokes, to climaxing together during sex, our lives are intertwined and immortal. I will always do everything I can to make her feel as loved and invincible as she makes me feel.

Our relationship wasn't "love at first sight" but it definitely snowballed. I spent all our time apart thinking about her, and was always excited to catch up. In the beginning she had two nannies so it was easy to sneak off for a day and explore the surrounding beaches and wineries. Our love was blossoming and I remember feeling a different type of freedom that Con provided for me. She made anything possible and her easy-going, generous soul was nurturing my heart back to love, and restoring my faith in good people.

Before I knew it, I had fallen totally and hopelessly in love with her. And while at first it was hard for her to believe, I fell in love with her kids as she fell in love with mine. It was obvious we were meant to be together; we shared the same thoughts and ideals. We view the world in the same way. We want the same things from life, for us and for our children.

There was one major hurdle at this period of our lives… I was aware that Con was soon to leave for her European tour and it was approaching fast. I had offered to housesit for her, but that was before our crazy love had taken hold. As the deadline approached, Con suggested we join her. Aside from being totally overwhelmed with her generosity, my passport had expired and my boys had never needed one before. Con assured me we could all get passports on time, and within a week we were all on a plane to Europe.

Oh my god, right?!!!

All of a sudden my life had gone from lying paralysed in my bed for a year, with no firm direction, very few friends and a general apathy towards life, to walking the streets of Ireland with this amazing and somewhat famous lover, on a tour of Europe.

I have always said Con's fame is just the right level for me to handle. At the beginning I didn't realise exactly how big of a deal she was; but touring Europe, seeing the fans and witnessing the positive movement she created, was incredible. There is a very good reason for her fame – Con is smart, she's funny as fuck, she has a confidence and an inner and outer beauty. She makes you feel heard, understood and loved. She makes you feel like you're special and that no matter what the problem is, you can get past it. Con empowers everyone she reaches out to, and helps heal the deepest wounds. She tells us we can all help each other, and that's a movement I want to be a part of. It's a movement we can all be a part of, one that supports each other with love, kindness, empathy and non-judgement.

I'm very comfortable to play the supportive role in our relationship. Whilst in my youth I may have been more attention-seeking, now with age and possibly a little wisdom, I prefer to linger in the background as Con's star shines.

While we were in Europe I proposed marriage twice. The first time was a drunk, foggy memory, possibly in Ireland or maybe England. The second time, in Italy, was a little more serious. And I was deadly serious about this girl. I knew it was possibly too early... but when I'm with Con, everything just makes sense and it felt completely right. So when we returned to Australia I proposed again, in earnest this time.

The next shock to come was Con's pregnancy... it was not planned and caused a slight hiccup in our wedding plans, and future planned tour. Unequivocally, a baby was always in our future. We had spoken about it and agreed that it would unite us all. So honestly, I was really happy and I'm extremely proud of how well Con has handled everything she does, while having a belly full of arms and legs.

She is the most incredible woman I am now lucky enough to call my wife. Our wedding was just as amazing as every single day I spend with her. All she ever asks of me is to support her and keep things calm. And that's the easiest thing in the world for me.

The love Con and I have created between each other, and our children, is truly a dream and every day I wake and pinch myself to check I'm not still dreaming.

Oceans of love, Denim

I CAUGHT THE MOTHERFUCKER! IF WE GET DIVORCED I TAKE THIS WHOLE BOOK BACK!

The night before I married Denim we slept at separate places, probably the most traditional thing I've ever done; but I just wanted to be away from him so that when we saw each other we weren't sick of each other for the day yet.

All I thought about in the preparation for the wedding was what Denim would think of me when he saw me walking down the aisle. Would he be impressed with the dress? Would he be stoked at the look of his wife? Would he be excited to spend the rest of his life with me? Or would he freak out?

Denim is a sensitive guy; he thinks deeply about a lot of things and can be unpredictable at times. He's also a bit of a style guru, definitely not one of those guys who wants no input in what the wedding looked like. If he doesn't like an outfit on me, he tells me straight up. That's not to say I listen and take his advice, but on this occasion, I just wanted him to be really proud and impressed.

As I was falling asleep the night before, he sent me a text message: **I love you baby. So fucking much. It's killing me to not have you by my side. But tomorrow all my dreams come true.**

Thank you for finding me and loving my boys like you do. We just chatted about how much we love you and how lucky we are. Sleep well my princess... Tomorrow we redefine love to the world.

And like some stupid schoolgirl I took a deep breath, grinning alone in my bed, and hugged my phone close to my chest. It took any nerves I may have had away. All I need is him.

Getting ready was stress-free; my kids were with me, all of my bestest friends and my family. All with me to support what they all believe is the happiest they have ever seen me.

And then came our moment. Chet Faker's *I'm into You* is one of our favourite songs.

I was waiting behind some bush with my mammoth bridal party. People ask why it was so big, I question is why was it so small... I could have kept going, Denim made me stop.

Everyone we knew was there, waiting around a tepee, fresh flowers and gypsy rugs. Waiting for us to be as vulnerable as we get, for us to show them all how deeply we loved.

And I heard our song. And my kids started walking down the old woven carpet makeshift aisle, followed by my beautiful bridesmaids.

And I started walking; everyone started cheering me and whistling me, the energy was so thick you could cut a knife through it. Over the years I have cried to these people, they have held my hands, they have taken my kids for me, made us food. I never thought in a million years that they would be one day watching me shine this brightly, baby in belly, marrying my soul mate, with a tribe of children.

I looked ahead: there he was, waiting for me. He had the strangest look on his face. I got closer to him, I lifted his glasses and saw that he was bawling his eyes out.

"I just can't believe you're marrying me, you are so beautiful, just look at you."

I couldn't believe that I had made someone so happy, let alone the man of my dreams. I still can't believe this has all happened. We did it. We did in our way.

I could have lost everything, I nearly lost everything.

But everything is nothing without Denim.

*

Still a Queen is because I don't care anymore. I am happy and I am loved.

We women are damned if we do and damned if we don't.

Once someone told me that the reason so many people hate me is because I don't hate myself. I'm quite OK with who I am and that doesn't fit in with the apologetic martyr that women should be. So if I'm preaching less self-hate and that's going to make more Queens hated… What's the point? What hope do we have?

Receiving tens of thousands of messages, meeting with thousands of women all over the world and being followed by millions of women who share their support and stories with me has taught me so much.

Women need each other: it's not a want, it's a need. It's strength in numbers. We are put on this earth to connect. Babies learn to form attachments straight away, children connect with friends and as adults we seek love. Friends betray us and we trust again, lovers break us and we love again… and again, and again.

Because your purpose in life will continue to drive you towards it again and again and while you have your individual purpose, we all share a global purpose – to connect with each other.

You're going to be judged, hated, bitched about and ignored. Accept it and you're fucked; fight it and you're fucked. So if it's true as women we are damned if we do and dammed if we don't... how about we get comfortable with the damning?

Wear whatever you want.

Fuck activewear.

Don't brush your hair.

Sing all day.

Tell the mailman he's hot.

Eat that cake.

Kiss that woman on the lips.

Make up ridiculous stories to tell your kids.

Turn the TV off and make the kids dance for half an hour.

Get naked.

Fuck the routine.

Have hairy vag sex.

Quit, walk, run, leave him, stay, love him harder.

Paint on your walls.

See the beauty in everyone. Tell them.

You were born wild and you were born free.

Connect and connect and connect again.

And Love. Just keep loving.

Because you're gonna be dammed in style.

So all hail the dammed Queens, those with a past and scars and stretchmarks and trust issues and shame and guilt and that wicked, wicked sense of humour. Hail the lost Queens who search the earth wide-eyed for their kingdom to rule, the self-conscious and brave, the drunk and reckless, the calm and anxious, the damaged and tossed aside, the young and fearless and the old and wise, the guilty and the rule breakers.

She is the one with a story, a past, a burning light. She's fucked-up and hilarious and in a constant state of confusion.

But...

She is...

STILL A QUEEN

THANK YOUS

First and foremost I want to thank my lover, my husband. While I was writing this book he scraped poo off the back deck, he learnt to cook things he couldn't stand, he swallowed his socially inept ways and picked the kids up from school. All because my happiness is his happiness and the sound of my fingers on the keyboard, and me laughing at my own jokes, is music to his ears.

Every time I asked Denim if he was comfortable sharing something, he didn't even need to read it; he always said, "of course." He has no ego or desire to be portrayed in a certain light; the truth suits him fine. And I love his truth.

I'd like to thank my mother, sister and brother-in-law, all who systematically receive phone calls during my nervous breakdowns and have individual roles in calming me down. My sister agrees with my every complaint, my brother-in-law handles everything from a professional and business point of view, and my mum comes up with elaborate plans to defend her baby's honour. Nobody crosses an angry mum.

To my bestie, Annaliese, for just being a fucking legend.

I'd like to thank Cait O'Reardon for facilitating the publishing of this book. Her professionalism, experience and passion for reading have structured something that I am incredibly proud to put my name to. Cait has made this a simple and clear process, unscrambling my rambles and her guidance and patience gave this book life.

And finally I want to thank my children: Billie-Violet, Arlo, Rumi and Snow. They gracefully make the sacrifices that children with working parents make. They have learnt to share me with each other, with Denim and his two children, and with the public. My children are happy and free and kind and loved. They are my dreams come true. Along with my new children, the ones connected to me with love instead of blood, Sunny and Zeyke's gentle natures and pure souls are everything I ever wanted my children to become. They share their life with me, and in the public eye, with nothing but excitement and open hearts. These six kids along with Denim and the boy in my belly are my reasons for living.

And my Queens. Don't ever say thank you to me. I owe you so many more thank yous than you owe me. My life has changed so dramatically in the last couple of years.

I owe it all to you.

RAFIKI MWEMA

In January 2016 I received a message from a woman looking for help for a charity called Rafiki Mwema.

Rafiki is a Kenyan-based charity, run tirelessly and selflessly by co-founders Sarah Rosborg and Anne Marie Tipper, and a small group of staff.

They take in sexually abused girls and homeless, sexually abused, drug-addicted boys from the streets of Kenya. They move them into a therapeutic home on a farm, where they create healing, love and family for some of the world's most tortured and shamed children. They do this with nothing. Everything they have goes on these children; every month they are short, every month they go without, but they keep going.

I immediately wanted to work with them and posted about what they were doing on my Facebook page.

In March 2016 they came to me wanting help to build a house on the farm for the teenage girls, to get them out of a rental in town that posed too many dangers. They needed $70,000. I put it to the Queens on Facebook and within 48 hours we had raised over $180,000. The power of Queens coming together was obvious.

With these funds we built a home for the teenagers and it was named "The Queens Castle". With the extra money raised we also built a smaller home for the babies of the family. A quiet place to have one-on-one therapy for the smallest and newest members of the family.

When writing *Like A Queen* we decided that $1 from every book would go to Rafiki Mwema to build the same housing for the teenage boys. By March 2017 $170,000 had been donated, and this house is currently being built.

Still a Queen will of course do the same. We now need a house for our baby boys, so they can be away from the bigger ones to find their feet in the newfound safety of Rafiki Mwema.

Just by buying this book you have contributed to the safety of a little boy, who without Rafiki Mwema would be walked past on the street, discarded and invisible.Welcome to the Rafiki Mwema family.

For more information please visit
www.rafikimwema.com:
there are plenty of amazing children to sponsor.